Writing the Critical Essay

The War in Afghanistan

An OPPOSING **VIEWPOINTS**® Guide

Lauri S. Scherer, *Book Editor*

OPPOSING
VIEWPOINTS®
SERIES

GREENHAVEN PRESS
A part of Gale, Cengage Learning

GALE
CENGAGE Learning®

Detroit • New York • San Francisco • New Haven, Conn • Waterville, Maine • London

Elizabeth Des Chenes, *Director, Publishing Solutions*

© 2012 Greenhaven Press, a part of Gale, Cengage Learning

Gale and Greenhaven Press are registered trademarks used herein under license.

For more information, contact:
Greenhaven Press
27500 Drake Rd.
Farmington Hills, MI 48331-3535
Or you can visit our Internet site at gale.cengage.com

For product information and technology assistance, contact us at

Gale Customer Support, 1-800-877-4253
For permission to use material from this text or product, submit all requests online at www.cengage.com/permissions

Further permissions questions can be e-mailed to permissionrequest@cengage.com

Articles in Greenhaven Press anthologies are often edited for length to meet page requirements. In addition, original titles of these works are changed to clearly present the main thesis and to explicitly indicate the author's opinion. Every effort is made to ensure that Greenhaven Press accurately reflects the original intent of the authors. Every effort has been made to trace the owners of copyrighted material.

Cover image © Oleg Zabielin/Shutterstock.com.

LIBRARY OF CONGRESS CATALOGING-IN-PUBLICATION DATA

The war in Afghanistan / Lauri S. Scherer, book editor.
    p. cm. -- (Writing the critical essay : an opposing viewpoints guide)
Includes bibliographical references and index.
    ISBN 978-0-7377-5911-2 (hardcover)
    1. Afghan War, 2001- 2. Academic writing--Handbooks, manuals, etc. 3. Essay--Authorship--Handbooks, manuals, etc. 4. Criticism--Authorship--Handbooks, manuals, etc. I. Scherer, Lauri S.
    DS371.412.W355 2012
    958.104'7--dc23

    2011051015

Printed in the United States of America
1 2 3 4 5 6 7 16 15 14 13 12

CONTENTS

Examining the state of writing and how it is taught in the United States was the official purpose of the National Commission on Writing in America's Schools and Colleges. The commission, made up of teachers, school administrators, business leaders, and college and university presidents, released its first report in 2003. "Despite the best efforts of many educators," commissioners argued, "writing has not received the full attention it deserves." Among the findings of the commission was that most fourth-grade students spent less than three hours a week writing, that three-quarters of high school seniors never receive a writing assignment in their history or social studies classes, and that more than 50 percent of first-year students in college have problems writing error-free papers. The commission called for a "cultural sea change" that would increase the emphasis on writing for both elementary and secondary schools. These conclusions have made some educators realize that writing must be emphasized in the curriculum. As colleges are demanding an ever-higher level of writing proficiency from incoming students, schools must respond by making students more competent writers. In response to these concerns, the SAT, an influential standardized test used for college admissions, required an essay for the first time in 2005.

Books in the Writing the Critical Essay: An Opposing Viewpoints Guide series use the patented Opposing Viewpoints format to help students learn to organize ideas and arguments and to write essays using common critical writing techniques. Each book in the series focuses on a particular type of essay writing—including expository, persuasive, descriptive, and narrative—that students learn while being taught both the five-paragraph essay as well as longer pieces of writing that have an opinionated focus. These guides include everything necessary to help students research, outline, draft, edit, and ultimately write successful essays across the curriculum, including essays for the SAT.

Using Opposing Viewpoints

This series is inspired by and builds upon Greenhaven Press's acclaimed Opposing Viewpoints series. As in the parent series, each book in the Writing the Critical Essay series focuses on a timely and controversial social issue that provides lots of opportunities for creating thought-provoking essays. The first section of each volume begins with a brief introductory essay that provides context for the opposing viewpoints that follow. These articles are chosen for their accessibility and clearly stated views. The thesis of each article is made explicit in the article's title and is accentuated by its pairing with an opposing or alternative view. These essays are both models of persuasive writing techniques and valuable research material that students can mine to write their own informed essays. Guided reading and discussion questions help lead students to key ideas and writing techniques presented in the selections.

The second section of each book begins with a preface discussing the format of the essays and examining characteristics of the featured essay type. Model five-paragraph and longer essays then demonstrate that essay type. The essays are annotated so that key writing elements and techniques are pointed out to the student. Sequential, step-by-step exercises help students construct and refine thesis statements; organize material into outlines; analyze and try out writing techniques; write transitions, introductions, and conclusions; and incorporate quotations and other researched material. Ultimately, students construct their own compositions using the designated essay type.

The third section of each volume provides additional research material and writing prompts to help the student. Additional facts about the topic of the book serve as a convenient source of supporting material for essays. Other features help students go beyond the book for their research. Like other Greenhaven Press books, each book in the Writing the Critical Essay series includes bibliographic listings of relevant periodical articles, books, websites, and organizations to contact.

Writing the Critical Essay: An Opposing Viewpoints Guide will help students master essay techniques that can be used in any discipline.

America's Longest War

The war in Afghanistan has reached two somber milestones: On June 7, 2010, after persisting for eight years and eight months, it officially became the longest war in American history. Then, a little over a year later, on October 7, 2011, the United States marked the ten-year anniversary of war there, a commemoration that was as solemn as it was sobering. Both the war's ten-year anniversary and its designation as the longest war in American history have led policy makers, analysts, and American families to reflect on how it compares with America's second-longest military effort, the Vietnam War.

The war in Afghanistan completed its 104th month in June 2010, surpassing the Vietnam War, which officially lasted 103 months and which at the time seemed extremely long, given that the two previous wars—the Korean War, which began in 1950, and World War II, which the United States had entered in 1941—had lasted just 37 months and 44 months, respectively. Other notable conflicts were short by comparison, too: The Iraq War, for example, lasted 86 months, while the Revolutionary and Civil War lasted 81 months and 48 months, respectively.

When the war in Afghanistan outlived the Vietnam War, it unleashed a barrage of comparisons between the two experiences. In some ways, the conflicts are similar: Both stretched over multiple presidencies, fell out of favor with the general public, diverted resources away from domestic needs, and bogged down the military in an environmentally harsh area of the world with which it was culturally unfamiliar and, in which, at least in some places, it was deeply disliked. The word *quagmire*—a precarious, quicksand-like situation from which extraction is difficult—has been used to describe both conflicts, as has the term *mission creep*, which refers to a war effort that has evolved beyond its originally stated goals. "The comparisons roll off tongues easily in Washington these days: Vietnam and Afghanistan, both home to far-away, maddeningly intractable struggles," writes the *Wall Street Journal*'s Gerald F. Seib. "The former became a quagmire that devoured a presidency; might the latter as well?"[1]

Yet in important ways, the conflicts are different. The Vietnam War was born out of an ideological struggle and a policy of containment: It was intended to prevent Communists from gaining power in Southeast Asia. The Vietnam War was a proxy battle of the Cold War, the decades-long standoff between the Communist Soviet Union and the capitalist, democratic United States in which the two superpowers vied for influence around the globe.

The war in Afghanistan, on the other hand, began as a swift response to a violent attack that defined a generation: The September 11, 2001, terrorist attacks, in which terrorists hijacked jetliners and flew them into buildings in New York and Washington, DC, killing nearly three thousand civilians. The September 11 attacks were planned and executed by Osama bin Laden's terrorist group al Qaeda, which was sheltered by the Taliban, the Islamic fundamentalist group that ruled Afghanistan. President George W. Bush demanded that the Taliban hand over the terrorists or face war. "Deliver to United States authorities all the leaders of Al Qaida who hide in your land," said Bush on September 20, 2001. "These demands are not open to negotiation or discussion. . . . Hand over the terrorists, or [you] will share in their fate."[2] When the Taliban refused, the United States invaded. The very different beginnings to each conflict are among the critical ways in which they do not resemble each other.

Another way in which the two conflicts differ is in the number of American lives they have claimed. After ten years of war, more than eighteen hundred American soldiers had died fighting in Afghanistan. Though each of those deaths was mourned, Vietnam left tens of thousands more families grieving loved ones: More than fifty-eight thousand Americans died in that conflict. The relatively low number of American casualties in the former is due to the fact that in Afghanistan, soldiers fight Taliban insurgents—small, guerilla forces that rely on the element of surprise and the deadliness of suicide attacks—rather than the large scale manpower and weaponry employed by an army.

In Vietnam, the insurgents' equivalent was the Viet Cong, also a guerilla fighting force. But the Viet Cong were supported by the North Vietnamese Army, which made them better armed and more deadly. "From a military perspective and a counterinsurgency perspective, the most important difference is that there is no North Vietnam in this equation," says Frederick W. Kagan, an Afghanistan analyst at the American Enterprise Institute. "Yes, it's true that Pakistan provides some sanctuary and support [to the Afghan insurgents]. But the thing that brought down South Vietnam in the end was the North Vietnamese army."[3]

The way in which the war in Afghanistan has played out, however, reminds many of the Vietnam War. Like Vietnam, Afghanistan features corrupt, weak leaders that are propped up by the United States; it has cost the United States billions of dollars yet has not achieved its goals in a tenable, permanent way. A revolving door of US military commanders has led a mission that lacks clearly defined goals and an end date, and areas of the country cleared of insurgents have been known to fall back under their control within months of having been secured. "It all sounds familiar," says Theodore Sorenson, who advised President John F. Kennedy during the Vietnam War. "Afghanistan isn't threatening to become another Vietnam. It already is,"[4] Sorenson asserts.

Robert Wright, of the New America Foundation, agrees. "The Afghanistan war is as bad as the Vietnam War except for the ways in which it's worse," he writes. Wright argues that in addition to wasting resources and lives, the war in Afghanistan has inspired legions of new terrorists to attack the United States, which was not an issue in the Vietnam War. "Just as Al Qaeda planned, [the war] empowers the narrative of terrorist recruiters.

. . . Could we please stop doing al Qaeda's work for it?"[5] Sorenson, Wright, and others are among the voices calling for American leaders to learn from the mistakes the United States made in Vietnam and apply the lessons to Afghanistan, before more lives and resources are wasted.

That Afghanistan has become America's longest war, and what that means for both nations, are among the many issues explored in *Writing the Critical Essay: The War in Afghanistan*. Readers will also consider arguments about whether the war is winnable, whether the United States should make a long-term commitment to Afghanistan, and whether the United States is justified in being there now that its original principal target, Osama bin Laden, has been killed. These issues are explored in passionately argued viewpoints and model essays. Thought-provoking writing exercises and step-by-step instructions help readers conduct their own interviews and write their own five-paragraph descriptive essays on the topic.

Notes

1. Gerald F. Seib, "Memories of Vietnam Haunt War, but Scarcely Apply," *Wall Street Journal*, October 26, 2009. http://online.wsj.com/article/SB125633512948004625 .html.
2. George W. Bush, "Address to a Joint Session of Congress and the American People," Washington, DC, September 20, 2001. http://georgewbush-whitehouse.archives.gov /news/releases/2001/09/20010920-8.html.
3. Quoted in Seib, "Memories of Vietnam Haunt War, but Scarcely Apply."
4. Theodore Sorenson, "America's Next Unwinnable War," *The Daily Beast*, October 30, 2009. www.thedaily beast.com/blogs-and-stories/2009-10-30/americas -next-unwinnable-war/.
5. Robert Wright, "Worse than Vietnam," *New York Times*, November 23, 2010. http://opinionator.blogs.nytimes .com/2010/11/23/afghanistan-and-vietnam/.

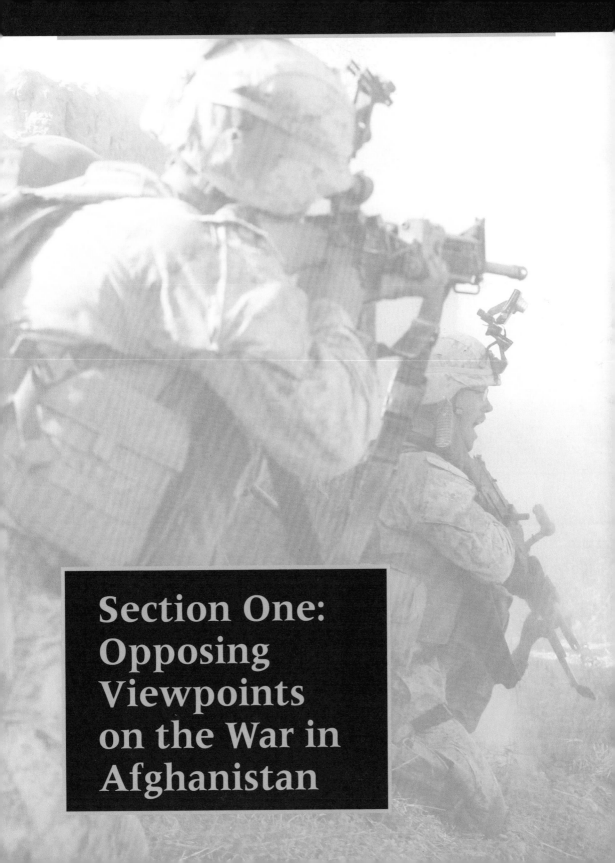

**Section One:
Opposing
Viewpoints
on the War in
Afghanistan**

The War in Afghanistan Is Winnable

Frederick W. Kagan and Kimberly Kagan

In the following essay Frederick W. Kagan and Kimberly Kagan argue that the war in Afghanistan is winnable. They explain that a new commander—General David Petraeus—has taken control of forces, and they think he will bring success to operations in Afghanistan. They also explain that President Barack Obama has committed thousands more troops to the region, which gives the authors hope that the United States will have the manpower it needs to make large-scale progress there. The Kagans conclude that years of war have taught international forces critical lessons that will help them succeed in Afghanistan. They say the war has had several important triumphs that will ultimately lead to overall victory.

Frederick W. Kagan is a contributing editor to the *Weekly Standard* and is director of the Critical Threats Project at the American Enterprise Institute. Kimberly Kagan is president of the Institute for the Study of War.

Consider the following questions:

1. What are at least three things the authors say General Stanley McChrystal achieved in Afghanistan before being replaced by General David Petraeus?
2. What was the region of Marjah like around 2009, as described by the Kagans?
3. Why is the city of Kandahar so important to winning the war in Afghanistan?

Frederick W. Kagan and Kimberly Kagan, "A Winnable War," *Weekly Standard*, v. 15, no. 40, July 5, 2010. www.weeklystandard.com.

Success in Afghanistan is possible. The policy that President [Barack] Obama announced in December [2009] and firmly reiterated last week [in July 2010] is sound. So is the strategy that General Stanley McChrystal devised last summer and has been implementing this year. There have been setbacks and disappointments during this campaign, and adjustments will likely be necessary. These are inescapable in war. Success is not by any means inevitable. Enemies adapt and spoilers spoil. But both panic and despair are premature.

The coalition has made significant military progress against the Taliban, and will make more progress as the last surge forces arrive in August. Although military progress is insufficient by itself to resolve the conflict, it is a vital precondition. As the *New York Times* editors recently noted, "Until the insurgents are genuinely bloodied, they will keep insisting on a full restoration of their repressive power." General David Petraeus knows how to bloody insurgents—and he also knows how to support and encourage political development and conflict resolution. He takes over the mission with the renewed support of the White House.

Enormous Progress Has Been Made

Neither the recent setbacks nor the manner of McChrystal's departure should be allowed to obscure the enormous progress he has made in setting conditions for successful campaigns over the next two years. The internal, structural changes he made have revolutionized the ability of the International Security Assistance Force (ISAF) to conduct counterinsurgency operations. He oversaw the establishment of a three-star NATO [North Atlantic Treaty Organization] training command that has accelerated both the expansion and the qualitative improvement of the Afghan National Security Forces [ANSP] in less than a year. He introduced a program of partnering ISAF units and headquarters with Afghan forces that had worked wonders in Iraq—and he improved on it. He oversaw the

US general Stanley McChrystal devised a strategy to eliminate Taliban strongholds in Marjah and Kandahar in May 2010.

introduction of a three-star operational headquarters to develop and coordinate countrywide campaign plans. He has managed the massive planning and logistical burden of receiving the influx of surge forces and putting them immediately to use in a country with little infrastructure.

While undertaking these enormous tasks of internal reorganization, he has also taken the fight to the enemy. The controversies about his restrictions on the operations of Special Forces and rules of engagement that limit the use of destructive force in inhabited areas have obscured the fact that both Special Forces and conventional forces have been fighting harder than ever before and disrupting and seriously damaging enemy networks and strongholds. Targeted operations against Taliban networks have increased significantly during McChrystal's tenure, and the Taliban's ability to operate comfortably in Afghanistan has been greatly reduced. ISAF forces have killed, captured, or driven off numerous Taliban shadow governors and military commanders. They have pushed into areas the Taliban had controlled and eliminated safe-havens.

The Case of Marjah

The story of Marjah is particularly illustrative. Before this year, Marjah was a Taliban sanctuary, command-and-control node, and staging area. Taliban fighters based there had been able to support operations against ISAF and coalition forces throughout Helmand Province. Lasting progress in Helmand was simply not possible without clearing Marjah. McChrystal cleared it. The Taliban naturally are trying to regain control of it. ISAF and the ANSF are trying to prevent them.

The attempt to import "governance" rapidly into the area is faltering, which is not surprising considering the haste with which the operation was conducted (driven at least partly by the perceived pressure of the president's July 2011 timeline). The attempt was also ill-conceived. Governance plans for Marjah emphasized extending the influence of the central government to an area that supported insurgents precisely because it saw the central government as threatening and predatory. Although ISAF persuaded [Afghan] President Hamid Karzai to remove the most notorious malign actor in the area from power, Karzai allowed him to remain in the background, stoking fears among the people that he would inevitably return. The incapacity of the Afghan government to deliver either justice or basic services to its people naturally led to disappointment as well, partly because ISAF's own rhetoric had raised expectations to unrealistic levels.

The Enemy Is Losing Key Strongholds

The biggest problem with the Marjah operation, however, is that it was justified and explained on the wrong basis. Marjah is not a vitally important area in principle, even in Helmand. It is important because of its role as a Taliban base camp. It was so thoroughly controlled by the insurgents that the prospects for the rapid reestablishment of governance were always dim. It was fundamentally a military objective rather than a political one, and McChrystal made a mistake by offering Marjah as a test case of ISAF's ability to improve Afghan governance. What matters about Marjah is that the enemy can no longer use it as a sanctuary and headquarters. ISAF's military success there has allowed the coalition to launch subsequent operations in the Upper Helmand River Valley, particularly the more strategically important contested area around Sangin. The Marjah operation has so far succeeded in what it should have been intended to do. The aspects that are faltering should not have been priorities in that location.

Kandahar differs from Marjah in almost all respects. Kandahar City is not now a Taliban stronghold, although the Taliban are present in some force in its western districts and can stage attacks throughout the city. The Taliban had controlled the vital neighboring district of Arghandab until newly arrived American forces began contesting it in September 2009. The insurgents remain very strong in Zhari, Panjwayi, and Maiwand Districts to the west and south of Kandahar City, but they do not control any of those areas as completely as they controlled Marjah.

> # The Winnable War
>
> It is simply wrong to say that Afghanistan is a hopeless 14th-century basket case. This country had decent institutions before the Communist takeover. It hasn't fallen into chaos, the way Iraq did, because it has a culture of communal discussion and a respect for village elders. The Afghans have embraced the democratic process with enthusiasm.
>
> David Brooks, "The Winnable War," *New York Times*, March 27, 2009, p. A29.

As of 2011, the majority of Americans thought the United States would either definitely or probably succeed in achieving its goals in Afghanistan.

Question: "Regardless of what you think about the original decision to use military force in Afghanistan, do you now believe that the United States will definitely succeed, probably succeed, probably fail, or definitely fail in achieving its goals in Afghanistan?"

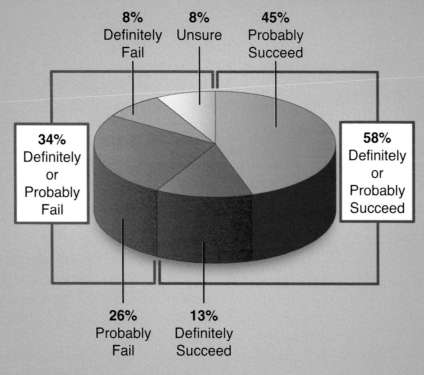

8%
Definitely
Fail

8%
Unsure

45%
Probably
Succeed

34%
Definitely
or
Probably
Fail

58%
Definitely
or
Probably
Succeed

26%
Probably
Fail

13%
Definitely
Succeed

Taken from: Pew Research Center, June 15–19, 2011.

An even greater difference is that Kandahar City and the surrounding districts are strategically important terrain. It is much too strong to say "as Kandahar goes, so goes Afghanistan"—the coalition could succeed in Kandahar and still lose the war. But it is very hard to imagine winning the war without winning in Kandahar. It is the most populous city in Afghanistan's Pashtun belt, the historical base of the Pashtun dynasties that formed and ruled Afghanistan for most of the last 250 years, and the birthplace of the Taliban itself, as well as the home of the Karzai family. It is also geographically important as the major city at the southwestern tip of the Hindu Kush and the junction of the roads from Herat, Kabul, and Quetta (in Pakistan). For all of these reasons, enduring stability in Kandahar underwritten by acceptable and effective governance is an essential precondition for success in Afghanistan in a way that stability in Marjah simply is not.

A Strategy for Success

The Marjah operation nevertheless offers important lessons about how to approach Kandahar. McChrystal had already rightly abandoned the idea of parachuting government officials into cleared areas around Kandahar before his departure. He was focusing instead on trying to get the government officials already in place to build local support for the operation. That effort, manifested by several *jirgas* and *shuras* (gatherings of officials and elders) over the past few months, has been faltering. McChrystal had recognized the problem before his departure, which is one reason he had announced a delay in the planned clearing operations around Kandahar. Petraeus now has the opportunity to revisit this approach to building local support for the operation and correct it.

It is too soon to say which of the various alternative approaches Petraeus will adopt or whether it will succeed. Learning, adapting, and trying different approaches are not the same as failing or losing. On the contrary, these are an essential part of success. American forces in Iraq experimented with a variety of approaches over years throughout the country before hitting on the right set of solutions. Under McChrystal's command, ISAF was moving through similar phases in Afghanistan much more rapidly. Since Petraeus has already shown his ability to explore alternatives until he finds one that works, there is reason to have some confidence that he will do so in Kandahar and in Afghanistan more generally. . . .

Success Is Possible

The problem in Afghanistan is [that] power-brokers are not engaged so much in tribal cleansing or death squads, but they do use their own private security companies to enforce order, sometimes at the expense of marginalized groups who fuel the insurgency. . . . A sound ISAF strategy would attempt to remove malign actors where necessary and possible, but also work to shape them and the environment in which they operate in ways that persuade or prevent them from engaging in the malign

US Marines engage Taliban fighters in Marjah, Afghanistan, in May 2010.

behavior that is fueling the insurgency and preventing stable governance from taking hold. Improving the way ISAF contracts with local companies—a process that has already begun—is part of the solution, but only part. ISAF will have to refocus its efforts at every level away from a binary choice between removing and empowering the malign actors, and toward the kind of nuanced approach that was successful in Iraq, appropriately modified.

There are never any guarantees in war. But the fact that efforts now will be led by General David Petraeus, with his record of judgment and creativity, is grounds for confidence that we can succeed.

Analyze the essay:

1. In this essay, the authors use facts, examples, logic, and reasoning to make their argument that the United States can win the war in Afghanistan. They do not, however, use any quotations to support their points. If you were to rewrite this article and insert quotations, what authorities might you quote from? Where would you place them, and why?

2. In this essay, the Kagans argue that a "doubling down" of more troops will give US and international forces the edge they need to win in Afghanistan. How does Hizb ut-Tahrir Britain, author of the following essay, directly respond to this claim? Cite from both texts in your answer.

The War in Afghanistan Is Unwinnable

Hizb ut-Tahrir Britain

Hizb ut-Tahrir is an Islamic political party active in several countries, including the United States and Great Britain. It opposes Western influence in Islamic countries, and its goal is to reinstate a broad, large-scale Islamic state that transcends national boundaries and ethnicities.

In the following essay, Hizb ut-Tahrir Britain argues that the war in Afghanistan is unwinnable and should be abandoned at once. It claims that the war is unjust, poorly conceived, misguided, immoral, and without any end in sight. It charges the United States and coalition nations with conducting an atrocious occupational campaign, and predicts they will, like others who have tried to conquer Afghanistan, fail in their mission. Hizb ut-Tahrir Britain argues that the war in Afghanistan fosters anti-American resentment and hatred, which fuels more terrorism than the war itself prevents. For these reasons and more, Hizb ut-Tahrir Britain concludes that the war in Afghanistan should be abandoned.

Consider the following questions:

1. What does the author say is known as "the graveyard for empires," and why?
2. How, according to Hizb ut-Tahrir Britain, does the Afghanistan of 2010 differ from the Afghanistan of 2001?
3. What percent of the total soldier fatalities in Afghanistan are shouldered by troops from the United States and the United Kingdom, as reported by the author?

"Executive Summary and Recommendations," *Afghanistan and Pakistan: The Unwinnable War,* special report by Hizb ut-Tahrir Britain, 2010, pp. 4–8. hizb -america.org. Copyright © 2010 by Hizb ut-Tahrir Britain. All rights reserved. Reproduced by permission.

A major sign of incompetence is a person who does the same thing over and over again while each time expecting different results. President Barack Obama and [now former British] Prime Minister Gordon Brown seem to be trapped in such an illusion. In 2001, when Western leaders ordered the invasion of Afghanistan, they set out their objectives for its occupation. They talked of bringing peace to the region, establishing a government which is accountable, promoting economic and industrial development, ending opium trade and securing the rights of the Afghan people.

A Decade of Disasters

At the end of the decade, the West has been unable to deliver in Afghanistan. Instead, the people of Afghanistan have been subjected to a brutal occupation, thousands of civilians have been killed and many Afghans have witnessed firsthand the West's empty promises of 'freedom' and 'human rights' when detained and tortured in Bagram and Kandahar. The [Hamid] Karzai regime, thoroughly discredited by ineptitude, corruption and dealings with brutal warlords, continues to be propped up by both London and Washington. The opium trade is booming and politicians with close ties to the West are alleged to be wrapped up in it. There is no economic or industrial development and despite pledges of billions of dollars in aid, there is little evidence of the rebuilding of Afghanistan that was promised.

After eight years the West has lost any form of moral authority to continue its occupation and its support of the widely discredited Karzai regime. There is no cogent reason to believe that they would even begin to make progress given another eight years. The neo-colonial mission in Afghanistan has failed. The West and its client regime in [the Afghan capital city of] Kabul have no legitimacy or credibility in the eyes of the Afghan people or wider Muslim world. This eight year long folly must now come to an end.

A Critical Lack of Strategy

Although it was their warmongering predecessors who launched the Afghan war, both Obama and Brown have decided to double down and have devoted more resources in a vain attempt to "finish the job." But with no coherent strategy, an excess use of violent tactics coupled with gross incompetence, NATO [North Atlantic Treaty Organization] rule has led to Afghanistan being controlled by drug barons and corrupt officials. Far from being able to defeat [terrorist network] Al-Qaeda or the Taliban in Afghanistan, the war will cause more resentment and hatred especially in the Muslim world where the West's reputation is already in tatters perpetuating instability and chaos.

Yet after the defeat in Iraq, the continued failure in Afghanistan and being fully exposed under the war on terror, Obama and Brown are now engaged in an "undeclared" war in Pakistan to destabilise yet another country in the Muslim world.

This Hizb ut-Tahrir demonstration occurred in London on May 25, 2011, to support uprisings in the Muslim world.

Many Lives Lost

As of July 2011, more than 2,600 coalition troops had died fighting in Afghanistan. More than half of those were American soldiers.

Country	Number of Deaths
Australia	28
Belgium	1
Canada	157
Czech	4
Denmark	41
Estonia	8
Finland	2
France	70
Georgia	9
Germany	53
Hungary	6
Italy	39
Jordan	2
Latvia	3
Lithuania	1
NATO	4
Netherlands	25
New Zealand	2
Norway	10
Poland	28
Portugal	2
Romania	19
South Korea	1
Spain	33
Sweden	5
Turkey	2
United Kingdom	377
United States	1,689
Total	2,621

Taken from: iCasualties.org, August 3, 2011.

A False Narrative

This is because these strategies were not just hopelessly executed, but hopelessly conceived. The analysis of Western war strategists is that the Afghan war has been under-resourced due to the war in Iraq and this explains the resurgence of the Taliban. The proponents of the new strategy believe that the lack of troops has led the people of Afghanistan to lose confidence in NATO's ability to provide greater security, a pre-requisite for effective governance. . . . By regaining momentum, the West believes they can then build up Afghanistan's indigenous security forces to take over from NATO at some undefined future date. . . . This narrative ignores some key factors:

The War in Afghanistan Is Unwinnable

This war is unwinnable as America learned so painfully in Vietnam and has discovered to its cost since 9/11. Historically, nations such as the Soviet Union have tried and failed to win in Afghanistan and could not placate the Pashtun tribes. It is not without basis that Afghanistan is known as a "graveyard for empires". Furthermore, if the promise is that this war will provide extra security, it will fail to achieve this. British forces in Northern Ireland, India's occupation of Kashmir, Israel's annexation of Palestine have never provided an iota of extra security for citizens of the occupying country. Occupation naturally breeds resentment and hatred which leads to retaliation, continuing the cycle of violence and counter violence we see in the world today.

> ## Afghanistan Cannot Transform into a Democracy
>
> It seems impossible for the Western powers, however well-intentioned, to make Afghans what we want them to be. We say we want to confer freedom of choice, a fine idea. But what if that choice favours warlordism, corruption, opium-growing and the oppression of women?
>
> Max Hastings, "Don't Fool Yourselves—Afghanistan Is an Unwinnable War," *Daily Mail* (London), November 6, 2009. www.dailymail.co.uk/debate /columnists/article-1225626/MAX-HASTINGS -Dont-fool—Afghanistan-unwinnable-war.html.

Western occupation since October 2001 has an atrocious track record when it comes to governance. Afghanistan today is more corrupt than it was in 2001, it produces more drugs than in did in 2001, and it has less security than it did in 2001. It has a

President who rigged a sham election and whose family is notoriously implicated in the opium trade. After eight years, where much of the Afghan aid has been wasted in the pockets of private consultants and government officials, Afghanistan remains one of the poorest countries in the world. With this kind of lamentable record, NATO should not be allowed to run a small market stall, let alone a country with 28 million people.

War Is Not Effective

You do not need 140,000 NATO troops and 190,000 Afghan troops to defeat 100 Al-Qaeda operatives in Afghanistan. If the mission is to defeat the Taliban (a group that evidently had no role in 9/11 and who are not responsible for any of the serious plots facing Western capitals), then NATO should say so upfront and then prepare its domestic population for decades of conflict in the

One of the biggest obstacles to success in Afghanistan has been the opium trade and corrupt Afghan politicians, including President Karzai.

dusty Afghan countryside, which will cost their tax payers dearly. The fact is that the Taliban are an indigenous Pashtun community and have seen off foreign invaders for centuries. As NATO increases their troop numbers, they will also increase theirs. The Pashtun Muslims comprise 50 million on both sides of the Durand line [the border between Afghanistan and Pakistan] with strong tribal and ethnic linkages between people on both sides of the border. Hence, it must be understood that if NATO goes to war with the Taliban then they are effectively going to war with the whole of the Pashtun community.

No Viable Exit Strategy

The exit strategy assumes that even if they ever achieve operational readiness, the Afghan security forces will do NATO's bidding and are ready to fight the insurgency. It is clear from the increasing number of cases of Afghan security personnel turning their fire on NATO soldiers that they are neither aligned nor brought in and trust is already breaking down. Yet, if NATO has no viable exit strategy then it will preside over a permanent occupation which will increase fatalities as well as incurring hundreds of billions in additional costs. Furthermore, if the war escalates as it is likely to do, British and American forces will take a disproportionate amount of the losses. Total losses in Afghanistan in 2009 were 504, with the US and the UK responsible for 80% of the fatalities. Ignoring the US, the UK lost more soldiers in 2009 than the remaining 41 members of the coalition combined. The 43 nation coalition exists in name only, with 34 nations providing less than 1,000 troops and 10 (almost a quarter of the coalition) providing less than ten troops. If countries other than the US and UK such as France, Germany, Italy or Spain are only providing token forces now with significant restrictions on what they can and cannot do, they are unlikely to support any further escalation.

If Al-Qaeda is indeed the target of the West, then according to most experts they are largely out of Afghanistan, with operatives now in Pakistan, Iraq, Saudi Arabia, Yemen and Somalia amongst other countries. NATO and Western governments should therefore come clean with their own public on their mission, that Afghanistan is actually a base to project the war both into Pakistan and to spread it to the Arabian Peninsula and the horn of Africa. However, this kind of war requires significant resources—human and financial—a long term commitment and an agenda for perpetual war in the Muslim world for decades. . . .

Millions of people share our discontent with the war on Afghanistan and still hope at least, to achieve some good from this terrible episode. Nevertheless, we conclude that there are root causes of the problem in Afghanistan that have not been fully debated and that there are solutions to the conflict if only those who have goodwill and courage to act on them. . . .

We recommend a genuine end to the occupation of Afghanistan

Analyze the essay:

1. In this essay, Hizb ut-Tahrir Britain says the United States has no moral authority when it comes to the war in Afghanistan. What does it mean by this? Do you agree? Explain your reasoning.

2. Hizb ut-Tahrir describes the war in Afghanistan as an occupation. Do you think Frederick W. Kagan and Kimberly Kagan, authors of the previous essay, would agree with this characterization? Why or why not? Write two to three sentences on how you think they might answer. Then, state your opinion: Is the war in Afghanistan an occupation? Why or why not?

The United States Should Commit to Afghanistan for Several Decades

Michael Yon

The United States should dedicate itself to Afghanistan for the long haul, argues Michael Yon in the following essay. Yon, a writer, author, and war correspondent, thinks part of the reason the United States has thus far been unsuccessful in Afghanistan is because it has been unwilling to completely commit itself to the cause. He thinks the only way for Afghanistan to turn from a terrorist-supporting, drug-dealing, failing state is for the United States and coalition nations to "adopt" it, which according to Yon means instituting an education system, building an infrastructure, steadying police and military forces, and undertaking other long-term nation-building commitments. Yon suggests the United States should build permanent bases in Afghanistan to let the people know they will not be abandoned, as they have been in the past. Yon concludes that completely committing to Afghanistan for the next several decades is the only way to win the war there.

Consider the following questions:

1. What does the author say brick military housing conveys, as opposed to a temporary barracks?
2. What does Yon say will happen to Afghanistan if the United States does not adopt it?
3. Why does the author think the United States will succeed in Afghanistan where the Soviet Union failed?

I have developed a strong belief that the war [in Afghanistan] is winnable, though on current trends we will lose. . . . In my view, we need more troops and effort in Afghanistan—now—and our commitment must be intergenerational. . . .

Afghans Want Signs of Permanency

We ask Afghans for help in defeating the enemies, yet the Afghans expect us to abandon them. . . . Afghans don't like to see Americans living in tents. Tents are for nomads. It would be foolish for Afghans in "Talibanastan" to cooperate with nomadic Americans only to be eviscerated by the Taliban when the nomads pack up. (How many times did we see similar things happen in Iraq?) The Afghans want to see us living in real buildings as a sign of permanency. The British forces at Sangin and associated bases live in temporary structures, as do the Americans at many of their bases. Our signals are clear. "If you are coming to stay," Afghans have told me in various ways, "build a real house. Build a real office. Don't live in tents."

A great many Iraqis wanted assurances that we would stay long enough to help their country survive but were not planning on making Iraq part of an American empire. It thus became important to convey signs of *semi*-permanence, signaling, "Yes, we will stay, and yes, we will leave." Conversely, Afghans in places like Helmand tend to have fond memories of Americans who came in the middle of last century, and those Afghans seem apt to cooperate. That much is clear. But Afghans need to sense our long-term commitment. They need to see houses made of stone, not tents. . . .

A Child-Nation Needing Adoption

It's crucial to hold in constant memory that Afghanistan is the societal equivalent of an illiterate teenager. The child-nation will fail unless we are willing to adopt the people.

Boots on the Ground: The Plan for Troops in Afghanistan

The Obama Administration plans to gradually withdraw troops from Afghanistan until the end of 2012, and expects to be able to hand over control to Afghan security forces by 2014. Some argue that US troop commitment should not have an expiration date, while others think the United States should stay there indefinitely.

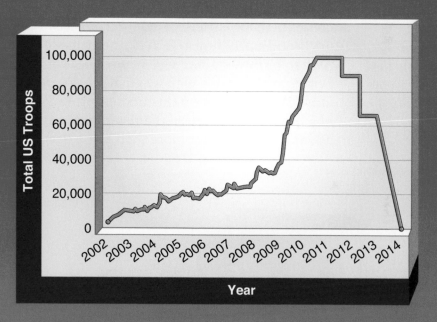

Taken from: White House Press Office.

Many Afghans clearly hope this will happen, though of course we have to phrase it slightly differently. Afghans are, after all, proud and xenophobic. They are not just xenophobic but also Afghanophobic. Most houses are built like little Alamos.

Big, Bold, Long-Term Action

Half-solutions failed in Iraq and are failing in Afghanistan. There will be no cheap, easy or quick compromise that will lead to long-term success in Af-Pak [Afghanistan and Pakistan]. Adopting a scaled-back counterterrorism approach would be like dispatching the potent but tiny Delta Force to the Amazon jungles with orders to swat mosquitoes. We could give the Delta troops every Predator and Reaper in our arsenal, yet 20 years from now they'd still be shooting Hellfire missiles at mosquitoes.

Gutting mid-level enemy leadership has been very effective in Iraq and Afghanistan, but only in a larger context. Using strictly a counterterrorism approach, we'll end up killing relatively zero mosquitoes—the Afghan birthrate alone will ensure that we never win—before coming down with war malaria. Counterterrorism in today's context remains important, but only as part of a broader strategy. Afghanistan was a special-operations playground for more than half a decade. Nobody

Construction crews build a road in Kabul, Afghanistan, with US funds. Any long-term commitment by the United States would involve rebuilding the country's infrastructure.

can argue that our special-ops forces were not given plenty of assets and discretion. They also got more than a half-decade of free passes in the press. Gen. Stanley McChrystal is asking for more troops, not fewer. We need to provide him with the resources needed to win.

If Afghanistan is to succeed, we must adopt it. We must adopt an entire country, a troubled child, for many decades to come. We must show the Afghans that together we can severely damage the enemies, or bring them around, and together build a brighter future. The alternative is perpetual war and terrorism radiating from the biggest, possibly richest, and most war-prone drug dealers the world has ever seen. Under that scenario, Afghanistan could become the swamp that harbors the disease that eventually kills Pakistan, leaving its nuclear weapons on the table.

Nation Building Takes Time

The renewed and better resourced American effort in Afghanistan will, in time, produce a relatively stable and prosperous Central Asian state.

Peter Bergen, "Winning the Good War," *Washington Monthly*, July/August 2009. www.washington monthly.com/features/2009/0907.bergen.html.

A Long-Term Adoption

Adopting this child-nation means more than building up Afghan security forces. Afghanistan cannot finance its police and army, much less the education system and vast infrastructure needed to fashion and fuel a self-sustaining economy. Its uncontrolled population growth stems from ignorance. Only through the spread of education and opportunity can narcotics production, criminality, warlordism, and fanaticism be eroded.

Finally, while it is important to learn from the Soviet Union's successes and failures in Afghanistan, close comparisons between Coalition activities today and Soviet efforts in the 1980s quickly become silly. The Coalition can succeed where the Soviets failed. For that matter, we should also remember that the Soviets failed in the "easy" places where democracy now thrives, such as Lithuania, Poland, the Czech Republic, Hungary, and other countries that are now helping in Afghanistan,

Iraqi police recruits train under the guidance of NATO forces. A long-term commitment in Afghanistan would include spending time and money to train and equip the Afghan army and police forces.

and where the U.S. is now welcome. I remember Poland, East Germany, Czechoslovakia, Romania, and others during the dark days. It is no wonder to me that the Soviets failed while freedom and democracy succeeded. People who saw [Czechoslovakia's capital city of] Prague then and can see it today likely will have great difficulty explaining the differences to the uninitiated. The Coalition in Afghanistan is largely comprised of nations that have suffered greatly in recent times. They get it.

We should adopt Afghanistan for the long term. If not, there will be perpetual and growing trouble. We can succeed in Afghanistan where others failed.

Analyze the essay:

1. To make his argument, Michael Yon describes Afghanistan as a "child-nation." Consider what he means by this. Do you think this is an accurate description? Why or why not? Do you think Afghanis might consider this an offensive description? Why or why not? Explain your reasoning and quote from the texts you have read in your answer.

2. Yon used reasoning, logic, examples, and quotes to argue that the US commitment in Afghanistan should be deep and long term. He did not, however, use any facts or statistics to support his argument. Using your school library or the Internet, find at least two facts or statistics that could be used to support his argument. These could be the results of an opinion poll or a demographic survey. Make sure the source from which the fact or statistic comes is authoritative and credible.

The United States Should Get Out of Afghanistan Immediately

James P. McGovern and Walter B. Jones

The following essay was jointly written by a Republican and a Democrat, each of whom serves in the US House of Representatives. James P. McGovern (D-Massachusetts) and Walter B. Jones (R-North Carolina) argue that the United States should immediately end the war in Afghanistan. They contend that the war is too expensive—it prevents the United States from bolstering its economy, creating jobs, providing health care for its citizens, and investing in other domestic improvements that have languished as the war has dragged on. They also say that the war has been ineffective—the original reason for the war was to catch the people who orchestrated the September 11, 2001, terrorist attacks, but according to McGovern and Jones, war is the wrong way to accomplish that. In their view, the United States has gotten sidetracked on a massive nation-building exercise that is bound to fail. They recommend withdrawing troops and ending the war immediately.

Consider the following questions:

1. At the time of the authors' writing, how many months had the war in Afghanistan lasted?
2. Who is Joseph Stiglitz and how does he factor into McGovern and Jones's argument?
3. What does the word *mystique* mean in the context of the essay?

No one, it seems, wants to talk about the war in Afghanistan. This week [in February 2011] the House debated a budget bill that is touted as reflecting new fiscal restraint, yet borrows tens of billions more for the war. In an hour-long State of the Union address last month, President [Barack] Obama devoted less than one minute to the conflict. Given the investment and sacrifices our country has made for nearly 10 years, the phones in our offices should be ringing off the hook with calls from those who are tired of being told that the United States doesn't have enough money to extend unemployment benefits or invest in new jobs.

But by and large, Americans are silent. The war wasn't even an issue in the November [2010] elections, which dominated the political discussion for much of last year. Perhaps it is because there is no draft and only a small percentage of our population is at risk. Or maybe it's because

Afghanistan is America's longest war. As of March 2012 it was ongoing for 125 months and cost more than 1400 troops their lives.

no one feels that they are paying for the war, which is being charged to the American taxpayers' credit card.

A Long, Bad War

Whatever the reasons, there is no excuse for our collective indifference. At 112 months, this is the longest war in our history. More than 1,400 American service members have lost their lives in Afghanistan; over 8,800 have been wounded in action. Tens of thousands have suffered other disabilities or psychological harm. The Pentagon reported in November that suicide rates are soaring among veterans; the backlog at the Department of Veterans Affairs had reached more than 700,000 disability cases, according to NPR [National Public Radio], including post-traumatic stress disorder.

Meanwhile in Afghanistan, our so-called ally President Hamid Karzai is corrupt. Transparency International recently ranked Afghanistan as the world's third-most corrupt country, behind only Somalia and Burma. The Afghan military and police are not reliable partners, and [terrorist network] al-Qaeda is someplace else.

Americans and Afghans Want the Troops to Leave

A drawdown is what the majority of the American people want. They want us to end America's longest war in history. They want us to stop spending $120 billion a year in Afghanistan, particularly when our heavy military footprint is not making Americans or Afghans safer. In the last year, we had the highest number of U.S. casualties, the biggest single-year spike in insurgent attacks, . . . an Afghan majority that says their basic security and basic services have worsened substantially, and majority populations in the U.S. and Afghanistan that want the troops to leave.

Mike Honda, "Time to Draw Down in Afghanistan," *Hill*, May 10, 2011, p. 32. http://thehill.com/opinion /op-ed/160079-time-to-draw-down-in-afghanistan.

Too Expensive and Not Worth It

Vice President [Joseph] Biden said in Afghanistan last month that "we are not leaving if you don't want us to leave." At the NATO [North Atlantic Treaty Organization] summit in Lisbon, [Portugal,] the president said that we're in Afghanistan for at least four more years.

But for what? Why do we need to sacrifice more American lives? Why must we continue to align ourselves with a government that commits fraud in elections? Instead, why aren't

Noble Prize–winning Columbia University professor Joseph Stiglitz testified before Congress that the wars in Iraq and Afghanistan will cost between 4 and 6 trillion dollars.

we using all our resources to go after the terrorists that murdered so many of our civilians on Sept. 11, 2001?

The new Republican majority in the House came to power in large part by promising to control spending and reduce the deficit. This war has already cost us more than $450 billion; combined with the war in Iraq, it is estimated to account for 23 percent of our deficits since 2003. Where is the outcry from the Tea Partyers and the deficit hawks? Fiscal conservatives should be howling that this war is being financed with borrowed money. Those who support the war should be willing to pay for it.

The War Is Bankrupting the Nation

And where is the liberal outrage? Those of us who are tired of being told that we can't afford green jobs, unemployment or health care should be screaming over our Treasury being used as an ATM when it comes to supporting the Karzai government.

To be fair, there are a handful of prominent critics on the left, center and right. But most Americans are silent about the enormous sacrifice our country has made in

Afghanistan's Deadly Crop

Afghanistan produces 90 percent of the world's opium, which is used to make heroin. The drug causes up to 100,000 drug-related deaths annually and bankrolls insurgents fighting US and NATO troops. Afghanistan's booming drug trade is among the reasons people believe it cannot be turned into a functioning democracy.

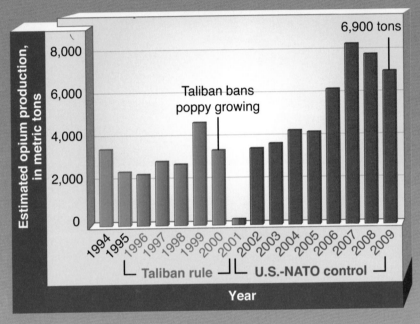

Taken from: UN Office on Drugs and Crime.

blood and treasure. They should be calling, writing or otherwise speaking out.

What are we giving up to maintain the status quo? Columbia University professor Joseph Stiglitz told the House Veterans Affairs Committee in September that the costs of Iraq and Afghanistan, including interest payments on the money borrowed for these wars and care for our wounded soldiers and veterans, is likely to total $4 trillion to $6 trillion.

Simply put, we believe the human and financial costs of the war are unacceptable and unsustainable. It is bankrupting us. The United States should devise an exit plan to extricate ourselves from Afghanistan, not a plan to stay there four more years and "then we'll see." This doesn't mean that we abandon the Afghan people—rather, we should abandon this war strategy. It is a failure that has not brought stability to Afghanistan and has not enhanced our own security. As the retired career Army officer Andrew J. Bacevich has written, to die for a mystique is the wrong policy.

End This War

It is easier for politicians to "go along" rather than make waves. But we were elected to do the right thing, not what is politically expedient. The discussion of Afghanistan shouldn't be about politics, which we acknowledge are difficult, but what is right for our country. And the right thing is to end this war.

Analyze the essay:

1. McGovern and Jones deeply disagree with Michael Yon, author of the previous essay, who argued that the United States should commit to being in Afghanistan for the next several decades. McGovern and Jones, however, think even four more years is too long. After reading both essays, which authors do you think made the more convincing argument? Why? List at least two pieces of evidence that swayed you.

2. McGovern and Jones are politicians—one is a Republican and one a Democrat—and they both serve in the House of Representatives. In what way does knowing their background influence your opinion of their argument? Are you more likely to agree with them? Less likely? Explain your reasoning.

Osama bin Laden's Death Should Lead to a US Withdrawal from Afghanistan

Barbara Boxer

Barbara Boxer is a Democrat from California who has represented her state in the United States Senate since 1993. In the following essay, she argues that the death of Osama bin Laden—the head of the terrorist group al Qaeda and orchestrator of the September 11, 2001, terrorist attacks—should lead to a US withdrawal of its troops from Afghanistan. Bin Laden was killed in May 2011 by US forces in Pakistan, after a nearly decade-long hunt for him following the 2001 attacks. Boxer reminds Americans that the reason the United States went to war in Afghanistan was to catch and kill Bin Laden—not to nation-build there or fight the kinds of insurgents that have developed in the years since. In Boxer's opinion, the goal of the war has been achieved, and thus the mission there is over. As a result, she concludes that US forces should be withdrawn from Afghanistan.

Consider the following questions:
1. How many al Qaeda members are likely left in Afghanistan, according to Boxer?
2. Who is Richard G. Lugar, as mentioned by the author?
3. According to Boxer, what percentage of Americans believe the death of Bin Laden signifies the end of the mission in Afghanistan?

In September 2001, when the U.S. Senate unanimously voted to use all necessary and appropriate force against those responsible for the attacks of Sept. 11, we knew our enemy: Osama bin Laden and his Al Qaeda network. Within a month, the United States began combat operations in Afghanistan, whose Taliban-led government had provided a haven for the terrorist organization.

Today, nearly 10 years later, we have accomplished what President Obama called the "most significant achievement to date" in our war against Al Qaeda: Bin Laden is dead. And according to CIA Director Leon Panetta, there may be as few as 50 members of Al Qaeda residing in Afghanistan.

Although we must remain vigilant in our efforts to defeat Al Qaeda and must continue our support for the Afghan people, there is simply no justification for the

Both Senators John Kerry, D-MA, chairman (left), and Richard Lugar, R-IN, believe US expenditures in Afghanistan are unsustainable.

continued deployment of 100,000 American troops in Afghanistan. This July, the president should expedite his promised withdrawal of our combat forces. Moreover, we should now set an end date for the U.S. deployment there.

As quickly as can be safely accomplished, American forces should be drawn down to a point where they are sufficient only to conduct targeted counter-terrorism operations, train Afghan security forces and protect American and coalition personnel. Richard Haass, the president of the Council on Foreign Relations, has suggested that 10,000 to 25,000 troops would be adequate to fulfill this mission and that this level could be safely reached within 12 to 18 months.

We have to be realistic about what we can achieve in Afghanistan. The notion that the United States can build a Western-style democracy there is a myth. Instead, we should focus on what we can and must accomplish: preventing Al Qaeda from threatening the United States, and supporting Afghans as they determine the way forward.

Recently, I heard an expert on Afghanistan state that withdrawing U.S. troops would be risky because it "reaffirms the regional perception that the United States is not a reliable ally."

I was startled by this statement. We did not go into Afghanistan with the intention of rebuilding the country or maintaining a large, permanent presence. Furthermore, the United States has sacrificed tremendously in Afghanistan. We are spending an estimated $10 billion a month there, and our total so far is almost half a trillion dollars. We have trained 125,000 members of the Afghan police and 159,000 members of the Afghan army, and spent an estimated $26 billion equipping them.

Mission Accomplished

Now that Osama bin Laden has been found and done away with, the ostensible reason for U.S. troops risking their lives in Afghanistan also is no more. . . . With the death of bin Laden, President Obama should rethink [his goal to withdraw troops by 2014]. What can be accomplished in the next three years that has not already been done?

Times of Trenton (NJ), "Osama Bin Laden Death Should Hasten Troop Withdrawal from Afghanistan," May 10, 2011. www.nj.com/times-opinion/index .ssf/2011/05/editorial_osama_bin_laden_deat.html.

Americans Want Their Government to Focus on Domestic Issues

A 2011 poll found that the war in Afghanistan was low on Americans' list of priorities. Most people wanted the government to focus and invest in unemployment, job creation, fixing the federal deficit and health care, rather than spending money and time in Afghanistan.

Question: "Which of the following do you see as the most important issue facing the country right now?"

Issue	Percentage
Unemployment	42%
Government spending	17%
The federal deficit	13%
Health care	10%
War in Afghanistan	**5%**
Gas prices	4%
Immigration	3%
Taxes	2%
Other (vol.)	2%
Unsure	3%

Taken from: Bloomberg national poll, June 17–20, 2011.

Tragically, we have also lost 1,576 American service members, and another 11,541 have been wounded, many so seriously that their lives will never be the same. A recent article in the *Los Angeles Times* detailed the extraordinary increase in the number of American military personnel suffering the loss of multiple limbs or devastating groin injuries.

The Obama administration has clearly defined our objective in Afghanistan: to defeat Al Qaeda, ensuring that it no longer poses a significant threat to U.S. national security. We must not allow this goal to be distorted or expanded. The truth is we can continue to disrupt and dismantle Al Qaeda with sophisticated intelligence and

Senator Barbara Boxer argues that once Osama bin Laden was killed the United States reached its war objective in Afghanistan and should leave the country.

targeted counter-terrorism raids, as evidenced by the daring special forces raid that killed Bin Laden.

Lawmakers on both sides of the aisle share similar views. Senate Foreign Relations Committee Chairman John Kerry (D-Mass.) has called our expenditures in Afghanistan "fundamentally unsustainable," and the committee's ranking Republican, Sen. Richard G. Lugar (R-Ind.), said Afghanistan "does not carry a strategic value that justifies 100,000 American troops and a $100 billion per year cost, especially given current fiscal restraints."

Furthermore, Americans are ready for our troops to come home. According to a recent *USA Today*/Gallup poll, nearly 60% of Americans feel the U.S. has fulfilled its mission in Afghanistan and should bring the troops home.

That is why I have introduced a bill in the Senate that would require the administration to give Congress a plan for redeploying our troops that includes an end date.

The United States has spent more years fighting in Afghanistan than it has in any other war in the nation's history. We have made progress on our core objective: crippling Al Qaeda. Now is the time for us to focus on

that goal and finish the job. We can do this while dramatically reducing the number of our troops serving in harm's way and reducing the burden on our taxpayers. We owe that much to our troops, and to the American people.

Analyze the essay:

1. Barbara Boxer quotes from several sources to support the points she makes in her essay. Make a list of everyone she quotes, including their credentials and the nature of their comments. Then, analyze her sources—are they credible? Are they well qualified to speak on this subject? Why or why not? What specific points do they support?

2. Barbara Boxer and Peter Cannon (author of the following essay) disagree on how important Osama bin Laden was to the war in Afghanistan. Boxer views his death as a significant achievement, one that should signify the end of US involvement in Afghanistan. Cannon, on the other hand, argues that in the years since the war began, Osama bin Laden became less relevant to the on-the-ground fighting. After reading both essays, with which author do you agree on this matter? Why?

Osama bin Laden's Death Should Not Lead to a US Withdrawal from Afghanistan

Peter Cannon

In the following essay Peter Cannon argues that the death of al Qaeda terrorist leader Osama bin Laden should not cause coalition troops to withdraw from Afghanistan. Bin Laden was killed by US forces in Pakistan in May 2011. Although the war originally began in 2001 with the intent to capture Bin Laden, Cannon points out that in the decade since, Bin Laden has become largely a figurehead, a symbol of a dangerous movement that continues to rage within Afghanistan. Withdrawing forces now would undo everything coalition nations have worked for. Cannon argues that although Bin Laden was the reason to start the war, fighting terrorism has been the rationale for continuing it. Since Afghanistan continues to be a source of terrorism and terrorist inspiration, he thinks the mission has not yet been accomplished. He concludes that it would be a mistake to withdraw troops based on this one achievement.

Cannon is the governance, strategy, and terrorism director at the Henry Jackson Society, a British policy organization that deals with issues relating to democracy and geopolitics.

The killing of Osama Bin Laden has heightened speculation about an accelerated US and British withdrawal from Afghanistan. Some have argued that the death of Bin Laden reduces the 'rationale' for the US presence in Afghanistan, while some who were against the US presence in Afghanistan anyway have argued that Obama should use his renewed authority in the wake of his success against Bin Laden to push through an accelerated timetable for withdrawal.

There is little logic to this argument. The killing of Bin Laden was a significant success in the US campaign against Islamist terror networks. It seems illogical to argue that this success somehow undermines the justification for this campaign, of which Afghanistan is a crucial part. It is difficult to conceive of the operation against Bin Laden in Pakistan being successful if it were not for the long US operation in neighbouring Afghanistan. It would also be naive to assume that the death of Bin Laden marked the end of Al Qaeda terrorism.

Bin Laden's Significance Has Waned

Bin Laden's death is unlikely to have any major operational impact on the fight with the Taleban on the ground, as Bin Laden's significance was, by this stage, as a symbolic figurehead of jihad [religious struggle] rather than a commander with any direct influence on Taleban operations. Yet those critics of the Afghan campaign who argue that there is no connection between the Taleban and Al Qaeda are mistaken. A Taleban commander in the northern province of Baghlan issued a statement saying that his fighters would "avenge the killing of Osama", adding: "Osama is the leader of al-Qaida and he is a powerful man in jihad. Losing him will be very painful for the mujahideen [jihadists], but the shahadat [martyrdom] of Osama, will never stop the jihad. We will continue our fight until we liberate our lands from the Kafirs [invaders]." U.S. Lieutenant General David Rodriguez explained that there were still Al Qaeda operatives in Afghanistan, saying: "We still think that there are just less than a hundred al Qaeda operatives in Afghanistan. But what they do is a cadre-type organization that helps out to bring both resources as well as technical skills to the rest of the Taliban fighting here." This is a small number, but it is still significant.

The initial goal of the US invasion of Afghanistan was to find and kill Osama bin Laden (pictured) and disable al Qaeda.

Leaving Now Would Undo Gains

Nor does the fact that Bin Laden was found in Pakistan rather than Afghanistan in any way call into question the justification for the NATO [North Atlantic Treaty Organization] campaign in Afghanistan. The reason—of course—that Bin Laden was hiding in Pakistan rather than Afghanistan, and that Al-Qaeda is now to be found primarily in Pakistan rather than Afghanistan, is not a change of heart by the Taleban but the presence of US and NATO troops. With Al Qaeda having relocated across the border into Pakistan after the ousting of the Taleban from power in Afghanistan, it would be naive to think that there is not a risk of Al Qaeda returning in greater numbers were NATO forces to leave the country prematurely. Aside from which, a premature withdrawal from the country would embolden other Islamist enemies of the West and send out the message that Western powers were easily defeated by violent resistance. As Bin Laden himself said of the Soviet withdrawal from Afghanistan:

> Using very meagre resources and military means, the Afghan mujahedeen demolished one of the most important human myths in history and the greatest military apparatus. We no longer fear the so-called Great Powers. We believe that America is much weaker than Russia; and our brothers who fought in Somalia told us that they were astonished to observe how weak, impotent, and cowardly the American soldier is. As soon as eighty American troops were killed, they fled in the dark as fast as they could, after making a great deal of noise about the new international order.

Dangerous Forces Remain

It would be disastrous to give this impression once again. There is no doubt that the struggle with the Taleban does have a wider international significance. One recent example of this was the seizure by British Special Forces of

48 rockets in the southern province of Nimruz, a shipment which had come from the Islamic Republic of Iran. Mark Sedwill, NATO senior civilian representative to Afghanistan, observed: "These rockets represent a step-change in the lethal impact of weaponry infiltrating Afghanistan from Iran."

[US president Barack] Obama and [British prime minister David] Cameron have been putting their faith in reaching a political settlement in Afghanistan which will involve negotiating with the Taleban. While negotiations with elements of the Taleban may be fine in principle, we cannot rely on this as our strategy, as it depends on the goodwill of the Taleban—good will which has been far from evident. We need to continue to aim for military success against the Taleban, if we are going to be able to negotiate from a position of strength. On the eve of his state visit to the UK, Barack Obama stated that peace in Afghanistan "ultimately means talking to the Taliban". But they show no sign of wanting to talk to us.

> ### The War Against Terror Is Not Yet Won
>
> British and American governments would be making a grave error if they concluded that bin Laden's death meant the Afghan mission was now concluded, and they could order their troops to pack up and return home. The war against Islamist militants will only be won when they no longer pose a threat to our national security. And that will not happen if we abandon Afghanistan to the Taliban, the group that provided bin Laden with the safe haven that enabled al-Qaeda to launch the September 11 attacks.
>
> Con Coughlin, "Osama Bin Laden Dead: War on Terror Is Not Yet Won," *Daily Telegraph* (London), May 3, 2011. www.telegraph.co.uk/news/world news/northamerica/usa/8488415/Osama-bin-Laden -dead-war-on-terror-is-not-yet-won.html.

Thus far, the Taleban has given no indications of being willing to negotiate. It was recently reported that MI6 [the British intelligence agency] has advised the British government that efforts to make contact with the Taleban have been unsuccessful . . . with the message coming back from the leadership around [Taliban leader] Mullah Omar "that they are not interested."

A statement issued by Taleban spokesman Zabiullah Mujahid to the BBC [British Broadcasting Corporation] put it clearly: "We do not want to talk to anyone—not to [Afghan president Hamid] Karzai, nor to any foreigners—till the foreign forces withdraw from Afghanistan. We are certain that we are winning. Why should we talk if we have the upper hand, and the foreign troops are considering withdrawal,

Question: *"Now that Osama bin Laden has been killed, do you think that the United States has completed its primary mission in Afghanistan and surrounding areas, or not?"*

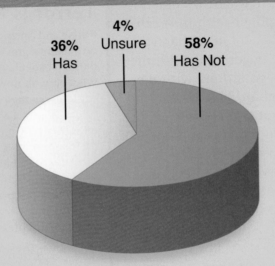

36%
Has

4%
Unsure

58%
Has Not

Taken from: CBS News/*New York Times* poll, June 24–28, 2011.

and there are differences in the ranks of our enemies?" There is little incentive for the Taleban to negotiate if we indicate that we are keen to leave as soon as possible, and that if they hold out a little longer we will soon be gone anyway.

Do Not Abandon Afghanistan

While the search for any kind of negotiated settlement remains a dead end, the military 'surge' strategy in Afghanistan is beginning to show signs of success. The programme to train the Afghan military and police force has reached the point where NATO is in a position to hand over control of a number of key districts to Afghan government control. They include Lashkar Gah, where the British military base of Camp Bastion is located. It would be wrong if this progress was to be undermined by US and UK forces being drawn down just as their efforts were beginning to pay off. As General Sir David Richards argued, the strategy must be given time to succeed. The withdrawal of troops should be determined by the military situation on the ground, not by arbitrary deadlines announced for political reasons.

That is why the recently announced withdrawal of 400 British troops, while a small number, is worrying. It seems to be an announcement designed to win domestic political approval, and one which forms part of a narrative of winding down our operations regardless of what happens rather than seeing them through to a successful conclusion. The death of Osama Bin Laden should in no way lead to an accelerated withdrawal by either British or US forces. Reducing our troop density is the biggest risk to our success. It would be a mistake to respond to a success against Al Qaeda by precipitating a failure in Afghanistan.

Analyze the essay:

1. Barbara Boxer (author of the previous essay) and Peter Cannon disagree on whether the death of Osama bin Laden qualifies as the end of the mission in Afghanistan. What do you think? What impact should the death of Bin Laden have on the war in Afghanistan? How significant was his death in terms of the overall war effort? Explain your reasoning and quote from the texts you have read.

2. Imagine you are the US president and have to decide whether to withdraw troops from Afghanistan based on the death of Osama bin Laden. What would you decide to do, and why? Describe your reasoning.

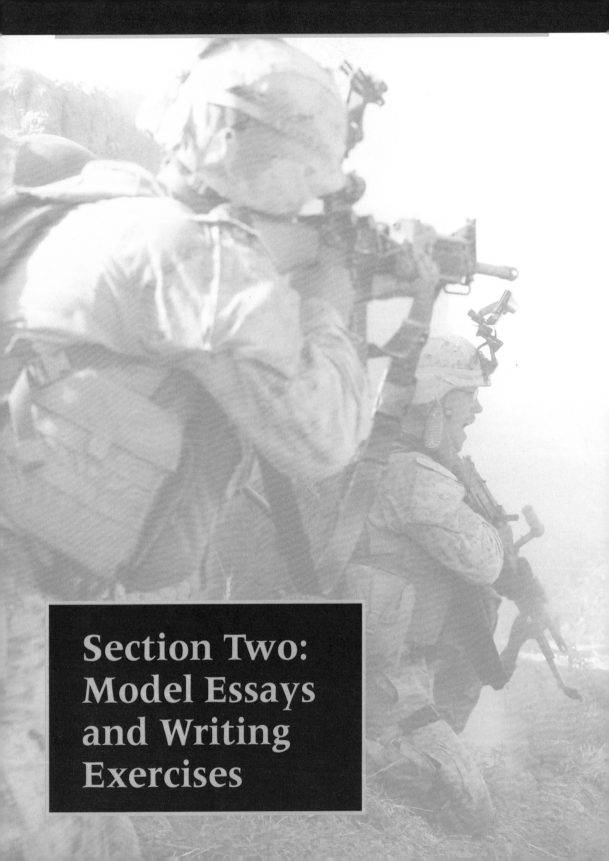

**Section Two:
Model Essays
and Writing
Exercises**

The Five-Paragraph Essay

An *essay* is a short piece of writing that discusses or analyzes one topic. The five-paragraph essay is a form commonly used in school assignments and tests. Every five-paragraph essay begins with an *introduction*, ends with a *conclusion,* and features three *supporting paragraphs* in the middle.

The Thesis Statement. The introduction includes the essay's thesis statement. The thesis statement presents the argument or point the author is trying to make about the topic. The essays in this book all have different thesis statements because they are making different arguments about the war in Afghanistan.

The thesis statement should clearly tell the reader what the essay will be about. A focused thesis statement helps determine what will be in the essay; the subsequent paragraphs are spent developing and supporting its argument.

The Introduction. In addition to presenting the thesis statement, a well-written introductory paragraph captures the attention of the reader and explains why the topic being explored is important. It may provide the reader with background information on the subject matter or feature an anecdote that illustrates a point relevant to the topic. It could also present startling information that clarifies the point of the essay or put forth a contradictory position that the essay will refute. Further techniques for writing an introduction are found later in this section.

The Supporting Paragraphs. The introduction is then followed by three (or more) supporting paragraphs. These are the main body of the essay. Each paragraph presents and develops a *subtopic* that supports the essay's thesis statement. Each subtopic is spearheaded by a *topic* *sentence* and supported by its own facts, details, and examples. The writer can use various kinds of supporting material and details to back up the topic of each supporting paragraph. These may include statistics, quotations from people with special knowledge or expertise, historic facts, and anecdotes. A rule of writing is that specific and concrete examples are more convincing than vague, general, or unsupported assertions.

The Conclusion. The conclusion is the paragraph that closes the essay. Its function is to summarize or reiterate the main idea of the essay. It may recall an idea from the introduction or briefly examine the larger implications of the thesis. Because the conclusion is also the last chance a writer has to make an impression on the reader, it is important that it not simply repeat what has been presented elsewhere in the essay but close it in a clear, final, and memorable way.

Although the order of the essay's component paragraphs is important, they do not have to be written in the order presented here. Some writers like to decide on a thesis and write the introductory paragraph first. Other writers like to focus first on the body of the essay, and write the introduction and conclusion later.

Pitfalls to Avoid

When writing essays about controversial issues such as the war in Afghanistan, it is important to remember that disputes over the material are common precisely because there are many different perspectives. Remember to state your arguments in careful and measured terms. Evaluate your topic fairly—avoid overstating negative qualities of one perspective or understating positive qualities of another. Use examples, facts, and details to support any assertions you make.

The Descriptive Essay

The previous section of this book provided you with samples of published persuasive writing on the war in Afghanistan. Many of these essays used description to convey their message. In this section, you will focus on developing your own descriptive writing skills.

A descriptive essay gives a reader a mental picture of the subject that the writer is exploring. Typically, descriptive writing uses the five senses—sight, sound, touch, taste, and smell—to help the reader experience what the writer has experienced. A descriptive writer carefully selects vivid examples and specific details to reveal people, places, processes, events, and ideas.

Using the Descriptive Essay

While an essay can be purely descriptive, descriptive papers written for the classroom are often persuasive or expository essays that use description to explain a memory, discuss an experience, or make a point. For example, in Viewpoint One, Frederick W. Kagan and Kimberly Kagan argue that the war in Afghanistan is winnable. To do that, they tell the story of the city of Marjah, which turned from a Taliban base camp into an area under coalition control.

Sometimes, descriptive essays are written in the first person (from the "I" point of view). Descriptive essays are a good format for the first person because details about a particular event or experience are well delivered through a person's memories, experiences, or opinions. Viewpoint Five, by Barbara Boxer, offers an example of first-person writing. Boxer draws upon her position as a senator to argue that the United States has no reason to be in Afghanistan now that Osama bin Laden is dead.

Descriptive Writing Techniques

An important element of descriptive writing is the use of images and specific, concrete details. Specific and concrete is the opposite of general and abstract. Descriptive writers should give their readers a fuller understanding of the topic by focusing on tangible details and by appealing to the five senses. See the accompanying box for examples of general nouns and their specific examples.

General and Specific Descriptions

General	Specific	More specific
vegetation	trees	maple
animal	fish	shark
grocery item	breakfast food	oatmeal
sound	screech	parrot's squawk

The use of metaphors and similes can also enliven descriptive writing. A metaphor is a word or phrase that compares two objects by identifying them with each other ("The sun was a great red eye in the sky"). A simile is a metaphor that includes the preposition *like* or *as* ("The sun was like a great red eye in the sky").

Some descriptive essays make use of scene and exposition. The scene is an element commonly found in fiction and other creative writing. With scene, a writer describes an event with moment-by-moment detail, often including dialogue if people are involved. With *exposition*, a writer explains, summarizes, or concisely recounts events that occur between scenes. Scene is comparable to "showing," while exposition is similar to "telling."

Finally, descriptive writing can be enhanced by including interviews conducted with people who have experienced an event firsthand. They are in a good position to offer detail-filled commentary on what a place looked, smelled, or seemed like. An example of how to conduct an interview and use it to write descriptively is found in Model Essay Three, in which the author interviews a soldier who served in Afghanistan. The soldier relays stories that are filled with captivating details about what serving in the region was like.

Tips to Remember

A descriptive essay should give the reader a clear impression of its subject. So, a writer must select the most relevant details. A few well-chosen details are more effective than dozens of less-related ones. You want the reader to visualize what you are describing but not feel overloaded with information. The room you are sitting in now, for example, is likely full of many concrete and specific items. To describe the room in writing, however, you would want to choose just a few of the most vivid details that would help convey your impression of and attitude about it.

A writer should also be aware of the kinds of words he or she uses in descriptive passages. Modifying words like adjectives and adverbs can enhance descriptive writing, but they should be used sparingly. Generally, verbs and nouns are more powerful than adjectives and adverbs. The overuse of modifying words makes the writing seem "wordy" and unnatural. Compare the phrases in the accompanying box to see the difference between wordy and concise language.

In this section, you will read model descriptive essays about the war in Afghanistan and work on exercises that will help you write your own.

Wordy vs. Concise Language

Wordy	Concise
bright green potted plant with thin leaves	fern
rolling around rapidly in brilliant untamed magnificence	dancing in wild splendor
she stopped extremely abruptly	she stopped
the best most amazingly wonderful experience	a fantastic time

The War in Afghanistan Has Improved Women's Lives

Editor's Notes The first model essay explores the way in which Afghan women's lives have improved since the fall of the Taliban in 2001. It is structured as a five-paragraph descriptive essay in which each paragraph contributes a distinct supporting idea that develops the argument. The author uses descriptive and persuasive techniques to convince the reader that even though problems still remain, on the whole, life is better for Afghan women.

The notes in the margin point out key features of the essay and will help you understand how the essay is organized. Also note that all sources are cited using Modern Language Association (MLA) style.* For more information on how to cite your sources see Appendix C. In addition, consider the following:

1. How does the introduction engage the reader's attention?
2. What descriptive techniques are used in the essay?
3. What purpose do the essay's quotes serve?
4. Does the essay convince you of its point?

Refers to thesis and topic sentences

Refers to supporting details

Paragraph 1

Look at Exercise 2B on introductions. What type of introduction is this? Does it grab your attention?

In April 2011, a woman in a fashionable, loose-fitting leopard-print headscarf browses through goods at twenty different shops in a women's market, the only and first of its kind in the Afghan city of Mazar-e Sharif. Another woman, this one in a bold green and red scarf, stands near her, sifting through crafts, beauty supplies, and photography equipment. The items are sold by women and the shops are

* Editor's Note: In applying MLA style guidelines in this book, the following simplifications have been made: Text citations in parentheses are confined to direct quotations only; electronic source documentation in the Works Cited list omits date of access, page ranges, and some detailed facts of publication.

owned by women. Though shoppers are modestly dressed, their hands are uncovered, free to inspect the quality of the fabrics and crafts; their faces are exposed, making it easy to talk with others. Some attend the market with their families and friends; others are by themselves. Women make purchases with money earned from their work as teachers, nurses, or shop owners. In most places this scene would be neither radical nor revolutionary, but in Afghanistan, it is an example of just how far women have come from.

> This is the essay's thesis statement. It gets to the heart of the author's argument.

Paragraph 2

For women, life under the Taliban was in every way oppressive. Until the Taliban was overthrown in 2001, women were not allowed to work, go to school, or leave their homes unless escorted by a male relative. Women were also required to wear a burqa, a thick, heavy robe that covers the entire body, and a *niqab*, which completely obscures the face. In addition to being shrouded while in public, the Taliban required that house windows be painted so no one could catch a glimpse of a woman in her home. "Women were beaten for showing a bit of ankle or wearing noisy shoes," reports Cindy Hanford for the National Organization for Women. "They could not speak in public or to men who were not relatives. They were beaten, even killed, for minor violations of these rules." Women's health greatly suffered under the Taliban, too—male doctors were prohibited from treating them, leaving most women with no access to medical care. "Female surgeons found it impossible to operate properly from underneath the burqa, with its limited vision, and some patients fortunate enough to receive care at all died because their doctors could not see to operate." (Hanford)

> This is the topic sentence of Paragraph 2. Note that all of the paragraph's details fit with it, or *support* it.

> Note how this quote supports the ideas discussed in the paragraph. It also comes from a reputable source.

Paragraph 3

More than ten years after the fall of the Taliban, however, women's lives have improved, especially in the urban areas such as Kabul and Mazar-e Sharif. The aid organizations Oxfam and ActionAid say women have much greater access to education, and 2.7 million girls were in school as

> This is the topic sentence of Paragraph 3. Without reading the rest of the paragraph, take a guess at what the paragraph will be about.

"For example" is a transitional phrase that helps keep the ideas in the essay flowing. Make a list of all transitional words and phrases used in the essay.

This type of quote is a *primary source* because it is from someone who personally experienced the changes the author discusses. Primary sources especially enliven essays.

This topic sentence both transitions from the previous material and introduces the topic of Paragraph 4.

Note how the author returns to ideas introduced in Paragraph 1. See Exercise 2B for more on conclusions.

of October 2011 (just a few thousand were enrolled under the Taliban). Women are free to go out in public, and some even own businesses. For example, Shakila Sharif owns a souvenir shop on a military base near Mazar-e Sharif. "My life is much better than it was under Taliban," she says. "I work here and nobody bothers me. I walk freely without a man escorting me around. God help us, she says, the future will be even brighter." (Qtd. in Martin) Gul Maky Siawash is another woman whose fortune has changed. She has even run for parliament, something that would have been unheard of under the Taliban.

Paragraph 4

Yet, despite much progress, women's rights undoubtedly have a long way to go. In rural areas, women have fewer opportunities, and rape, depression, suicide, poverty, illiteracy, forced marriages, and honor killings are common. In areas where the Taliban maintain a presence, women are threatened and terrorized. Twenty girls' schools were bombed or burned down between March and October 2010, for example, and at least 126 students and teachers were killed. Working women receive death threats from the Taliban, like this one that was sent to a female teacher: "We warn you to leave your job as a teacher as soon as possible otherwise we will cut the heads off your children and shall set fire to your daughter." (Qtd. in Khaleeli)

Paragraph 5

Although the situation for women is still perilous, Afghan women have at least a few bright spots to celebrate. As of 2011, according to Afghanistan's minister for women's affairs, 57 percent of women and girls went to school, and women made up 24 percent of health care workers and 10 percent of the judiciary. The mere existence of the women's market in Mazar-e Sharif is a marker of how much things have changed. US officials must do everything possible to make sure the improvements to Afghan women's lives are not undone once the United States withdraws its troops.

Works Cited

Hanford, Cindy. "Women's Lives Under the Taliban." National Organization for Women, Nov. 2001. http://www.now.org/issues/global/afghanwomen1.html.

Khaleeli, Homa. "Afghan Women Fear for the Future," *Guardian* 3 Feb. 2011. http://www.guardian.co.uk/life andstyle/2011/feb/04/afghan-women-fears-for-future.

Martin, Rachel. "Years After Taliban, Afghan Women Fare a Little Better," National Public Radio 22 Aug. 2010. http://www.npr.org/templates/story/story.php ?storyId = 129357288.

Exercise 1A: Create an Outline from an Existing Essay

It often helps to create an outline of the five-paragraph essay before you write it. The outline can help you organize the information, arguments, and evidence you have gathered during your research.

For this exercise, create an outline that could have been used to write "The War in Afghanistan Has Improved Women's Lives." This "reverse engineering" exercise is meant to help familiarize you with how outlines can help classify and arrange information.

To do this you will need to

1. state the essay's thesis;
2. pinpoint important pieces of evidence;
3. flag quotes that support the essay's ideas; and
4. identify key points that support the argument.

Part of the outline has already been started to give you an idea of the assignment.

Outline

I. Paragraph One
State the essay's thesis: Afghan women have made important gains since they were ruled by the Taliban.

II. Paragraph Two
Topic:

Supporting Detail i. Women were not allowed to work, go to school, or leave their home unless escorted by a male relative.

Supporting Detail ii.

III. Paragraph Three
Topic:

Supporting Detail i. 2.7 million girls were in school as of October 2011.

Supporting Detail ii.

IV. Paragraph Four
Topic:

Supporting Detail i.

Supporting Detail ii. The death threat received by a female teacher: "We warn you to leave your job as a teacher as soon as possible otherwise we will cut the heads off your children and shall set fire to your daughter."

V. Paragraph Five
Write the essay's conclusion:

Exercise 1B: Create an Outline for Your Own Essay

The first model essay makes a particular argument about the war in Afghanistan. For this exercise, your assignment is to find supporting ideas, choose specific and concrete details, create an outline, and ultimately write your own five-paragraph essay about the war in Afghanistan. Your goal is to use descriptive techniques to illuminate the topic for your reader.

Step I: Write a thesis statement.

The following thesis statement would be appropriate for an essay on why the United States should commit to keeping troops in Afghanistan for decades:

> *The Taliban and insurgent forces are simply biding their time, waiting until the last foreign troops leave to retake vulnerable areas of the country.*

The following essay would then explore the reasons the author thinks this statement is true. If you would like to pick a different topic, see the sample essay topics suggested in Appendix D for more ideas.

Step II: Brainstorm pieces of supporting evidence.

Using information found in this book and from your own research, write down three arguments or pieces of evidence that support the thesis statement you selected.

Then, for each of these three arguments, write down facts, examples, and details that support it. These could be
- statistical information,
- personal memories and anecdotes,
- quotes from experts, peers, or family members,
- observations of people's actions and behaviors, and
- specific, concrete details

Step III: Place the information from Part I in outline form.

Step IV: Write the arguments or supporting statements in paragraph form.

By now you should have three arguments that support the essay's thesis statement, as well as supporting material. Use the outline to write out your three supporting arguments in paragraph form. Make sure each paragraph has a topic sentence that states the paragraph's thesis clearly and broadly. Then, add supporting sentences that express the facts, quotes, details, and examples that support the paragraph's argument. The paragraph may also have a concluding or summary sentence.

The War in Afghanistan Has Worsened the Drug Trade

Editor's Notes The second model essay argues that bringing peace to Afghanistan has been made more difficult by the country's robust and dangerous drug trade, which ironically, was worsened by the war itself. Supported by facts, quotes, and statistics, it explains how Afghanistan's drug trade was unleashed by the 2001 invasion. It also explores how money from the drug trade fuels the insurgency. The author concludes that the war in Afghanistan significantly worsened the drug trade and made the job of peacekeeping more difficult.

As you read, consider the questions posed in the margins. Continue to identify thesis statements, supporting details, transitions, and quotations. Examine the introductory and concluding paragraphs to understand how they give shape to the essay. Finally, evaluate the essay's general structure and assess its overall effectiveness.

■ Refers to thesis and topic sentences

■ Refers to supporting details

Paragraph 1

US and international troops face many challenges as they fight to curb terrorism and bring peace and democracy to Afghanistan. One of the major challenges is the drug trade: Afghanistan is the leading global supplier of opium. Opium is made from poppy plants and is used to make the illegal drug heroin. Afghanistan's drug trade has become an enormous problem since the United States went to war, which is ironic because a booming drug trade was not an intended outcome of the mission.

What is the essay's thesis statement? How did you recognize it?

Paragraph 2

In 2000, a little over a year before the US invasion, the Taliban had actually significantly clamped down on the opium industry within its borders. Saying it was against Islam, they banned poppy growth and opium production. The Taliban ruled so tightly that farmers had little choice

This is the topic sentence of Paragraph 2. Note that all of the paragraph's details fit with, or support, it.

69

but to comply. Therefore, almost no poppy planting was done that year, and around the country, food crops such as onions or grains began to grow in abundance. Karim Rahimi, the UN drug control liaison in Afghanistan's Nangarhar Province, said at the time, "It is amazing, really, when you see the fields that last year were filled with poppies and this year there is wheat." (Qtd. in Robb, 143). As a result of the ban, the spring 2001 poppy harvest was the lowest on recent record for Afghanistan. By the time the United States invaded in October, opium production was close to zero.

What point in Paragraph 2 does this quote support?

Paragraph 3

When the United States overthrew the Taliban, it unwittingly jumpstarted the nation's opium industry. With little or no control in most parts of the country, no one could stop warlords from resuming opium production, which they did at a faster rate than ever before. According to the US military's Strategic Studies Institute, by 2004 the opium harvest set record highs; by 2006, production was double what it had been in the late 1990s. The United Nations Office on Drugs and Crime's (UNODC) 2011 *World Drug Report* confirms that Afghanistan remains the world's top cultivator of opium. It produces 63 percent of the global supply, and the industry generates $65 billion for Afghanistan each year. In 2011, opium crops were grown on at least 131,000 hectares of farmland, which was a 7 percent increase from 2010.

What is the topic sentence of Paragraph 3? Look for a sentence that tells generally what the paragraph's main point is.

What point in Paragraph 3 does this fact directly support?

Paragraph 4

The booming drug trade has hurt the war effort in several critical ways. According to the UNODC, drug money supplies Taliban insurgents and warlords with between $95 million and $160 million each year. More money is generated during years with particularly healthy crops. From 2006 to 2007, for example, the Taliban earned between $200 million and $400 million from the drug trade. These funds are used to buy weapons and other materials used to launch deadly attacks on coalition forces and the

This is a *supporting detail*. This information directly supports the topic sentence, helping to prove it true.

Afghan government officials who cooperate with them. Money from the drug trade is also used to pay Afghans to side with the Taliban, rather than with the United States and its allies. For example, the US military reports that the Taliban pay Afghan men up to $200 a month to fight on their side. They get this money from drug profits. This is a big financial incentive for Afghans: Police officers who work for the government are paid only $70 per month. To financially struggling citizens, it is much more profitable to work with the Taliban rather than against them. That the Taliban are able to buy Afghans' loyalty with drug money has been a major reason why ousting them from the country and installing law and order has been so challenging for coalition troops.

What point in Paragraph 4 does this fact directly support?

Paragraph 5

The United States did not intend to unleash a robust and dangerous drug industry when it overthrew the Taliban more than a decade ago. But war often invites unforeseen consequences and has uncontrollable chain reactions. It is painfully ironic that bringing peace to Afghanistan has been made more difficult by the country's robust and dangerous drug trade, which was worsened by the war itself.

Look at Exercise 2B on conclusions. What type of conclusion is this? Does it grab your attention? Do you like the way it wrapped up the essay? If so, why? If not, why not?

Works Cited

Robb, John. *Brave New War: The Next Stage of Terrorism and the End of Globalization.* Hoboken: Wiley, 2007.

"Afghanistan: Opium Winter Assessment." United Nations Office on Drugs and Crime Jan. 2009. http://www .unodc.org/documents/crop-monitoring/ORA_report _2009.pdf.

Exercise 2A: Create an Outline from an Existing Essay

As you did for the first model essay in this section, create an outline that could have been used to write "The War in Afghanistan Has Worsened the Drug Trade." Be sure to identify the essay's thesis statement, its supporting ideas and details, and key pieces of evidence that were used.

Exercise 2B: Examining Introductions and Conclusions

Whether an essay is a first-person account, an objective profile, or a formal persuasive paper, all pieces of writing feature introductory and concluding paragraphs that are used to frame the main ideas being presented. Along with presenting the essay's thesis statement, well-written introductions should grab the attention of the reader and make clear why the topic being explored is important. The conclusion reiterates the essay's thesis and is also the last chance for the writer to make an impression on the reader. Strong introductions and conclusions can greatly enhance an essay's effect on an audience.

The Introduction

There are several techniques that can be used to craft an introductory paragraph. An essay can start with:

- an anecdote: a brief story that illustrates a point relevant to the topic;
- startling information: facts, statistics, or shocking descriptive information that elucidates the point of the essay;
- setting up and knocking down a position: a position or claim believed by proponents of one side of a controversy, followed by statements that challenge that claim;
- historical perspective: an example of the way things used to be that leads into a discussion of how or why things work differently now;

- summary information: general introductory information about the topic that feeds into the essay's thesis statement.

Problem One
Reread the introductory paragraphs of the model essays and of the viewpoints in Section One. Identify which of the techniques described above are used in the viewpoints. How do they grab the attention of the reader? Are their thesis statements clearly presented?

Problem Two
Write an introduction for the essay you have outlined and partially written in Exercise 1B using one of the techniques described above.

The Conclusion
The conclusion brings the essay to a close by summarizing or returning to its main ideas. Good conclusions, however, go beyond simply repeating these ideas. Strong conclusions explore a topic's broader implications and reiterate why it is important to consider. They may frame the essay by returning to an anecdote featured in the opening paragraph. Or they may close with a quotation or refer back to an event in the essay. In opinionated essays, the conclusion can reiterate which side the essay is taking or ask the reader to reconsider a previously held position on the subject.

Problem Three
Reread the concluding paragraphs of the model essays and of the viewpoints in Section One. Which were most effective in driving their arguments home to the reader? What sorts of techniques did they use to do this? Did they appeal emotionally to the reader, or bookend an idea or event referenced elsewhere in the essay?

Problem Four
Write a conclusion for the essay you have outlined and partially written in Exercise 1B using one of the techniques described above.

Exercise 2C: Using Quotations to Enliven Your Essay

No essay is complete without quotations. Get in the habit of using quotes to support at least some of the ideas in your essays. Quotes do not need to appear in every paragraph, but often enough so that the essay contains voices aside from your own. When you write, use quotations to accomplish the following:

- provide expert advice that you are not necessarily in the position to know about;
- cite lively or passionate passages;
- include a particularly well-written point that gets to the heart of the matter;
- supply statistics or facts that have been derived from someone's research;
- deliver anecdotes that illustrate the point you are trying to make;
- express first-person testimony.

Problem One

Read or reread the essays presented in the first two sections of this book and find at least one example of each of the above quotation types.

There are a couple of important things to remember when using quotations:

- Note your sources' qualifications and biases. This way your reader can identify the person you have quoted and can put their words in a context.
- Put any quoted material within proper quotation marks. Failing to attribute quotes to their authors constitutes plagiarism, which is when an author takes someone else's words or ideas and presents them as his or her own. Plagiarism is a very serious infraction and must be avoided at all costs.

The War in Afghanistan Through a Soldier's Eyes

Editor's Notes The third model essay discusses the war in Afghanistan using a different aspect of the descriptive essay. It reports the firsthand experiences of a soldier who fought in Afghanistan. To do this, the author conducted an interview with the soldier, Jared Coulter*, who served in Afghanistan for nine months in 2009. The author uses descriptive techniques to convey some of the soldier's most enduring memories of his service. The information gleaned during the course of the interview allowed the author to get firsthand information, details, and stories about the experience. Because they yield these types of details, interviews can be a useful tool when writing a descriptive essay. More information about conducting an interview is found in Exercises 3A and 3B, which follow the essay. Note that this essay needed more than five paragraphs to adequately recount Coulter's experiences.

Refers to thesis and topic sentences

Refers to supporting details

Paragraph 1

Jared Coulter knew he wanted to serve in Afghanistan the first time he really thought about what happened on September 11, 2001, the day that terrorists attacked the United States. About a month after those attacks, which killed nearly three thousand Americans, the United States invaded Afghanistan, because the Taliban government had given shelter to Osama bin Laden, the terrorist leader who had planned the attacks. "Just thinking about the Americans who lost their lives and the terrorists who stole them from their families, you know—it really did something to me," he says. "I just wanted to try and right the wrongs that were done." Coulter enlisted in the US Army when he was

Coulter's comments lend the essay a personal feel. Make sure to integrate unique and interesting quotes from those you interview in your essays.

*His name has been changed to protect the soldier's privacy.

twenty-six years old and after basic training was sent to Afghanistan as part of Operation Enduring Freedom.

Paragraph 2

During his deployment, Coulter and his unit repaired roads, built new bases, conducted checkpoints, recovered equipment from dangerous areas, and led patrols. Soldiers on patrol were nervous and tense, Coulter remembers. During one patrol through a poor neighborhood in the city of Kabul, Coulter drove an enormous armored land rover through narrow, winding streets. Driving here was not easy. The roads had big potholes and ditches that made the land rover lurch back and forth, and Coulter felt like he was going to fall out. The vehicle stirred up a lot of dust, which obscured his visibility. The night was pitch black: with electricity scarce, there were very few sources of ambient light. "Just a light in a random window here and there; it's weird, like being in a blackout," he said.

Note how these specific details give you a very clear idea of what a night patrol must be like.

Paragraph 3

Eventually the road got so narrow and steep the soldiers had to get out of the vehicle and walk, their weapons drawn high. "I looked to my left and there were two guys watching us," remembers Coulter. "They appeared out of nowhere. Since we had no idea what they were doing, if they had weapons, were good guys or bad guys, we took no chances—we just threw up spotlights on them, just drowned 'em in light. Turns out they were harmless, and they scattered off into the darkness."

This is the topic sentence of paragraph 4. Without reading the rest of the paragraph, take a guess at what it will be about.

Paragraph 4

Other patrols were more saddening than tense. For example, Coulter remembers one patrol that took place during the day, in really hot weather. "You could smell everything in the streets," he said. "Garbage, stinky tubs of standing water, sewage—it was pretty potent." A large group of children surrounded the vehicle, begging the soldiers for chocolate, money, water, and even trinkets like pens and clipboards. "They were so sad, they were just in rags with these rundown shoes—some of them didn't even have shoes—and they were so dirty. But still children, you know? Still children." They ran alongside Coulter's vehicle for more than a mile before giving up. "I wanted to give them something, but you know, we couldn't, because then they'd come around all the time. If there was an attack or an explosion, they'd get hurt, or killed, and it was just better for them and for us if they weren't near us."

Paragraph 5

When on patrol, Coulter always looked for escape routes— places he could take cover in the event his patrol encountered enemy fire. He remembers one time when he was patrolling a row of houses that backed up against a stream. The stream was deep enough that he could have jumped in it to take cover if he needed to—but it was filled with human waste and sewage. He could see feces, toilet paper, and other trash floating down the water's current. "I wanted to puke just thinking about having to dunk my head in all of that," he said. "But I would have done it if I had to, I guess." Luckily, his patrol did not encounter any hostile forces that day.

When you interview a subject, choose to showcase only the most interesting, revealing, and personal quotes. Paraphrase more generic information that your subject tells you in your own words.

Paragraph 6

One of the scariest moments of Coulter's service took place on a morning he was supposed to have off. "But there never really is such a thing as 'off' when you're in the field," he says. As he and a buddy talked about how they wanted to spend their time, a huge explosion shook their building. "I looked up and saw windows falling in, glass was shattering everywhere. There was dust and glass chunks and wood and cement all over the beds." Coulter said that everyone in the room sprang to life. They immediately got down on the ground, taking cover where it was possible. He found his body armor and helmet, put it on, and braced for what might come next. "We didn't know if it was a rocket attack or what," he says. Within seconds his commanding officer came running into the room, yelling at everyone to get their equipment and move

Given the way in which they tell a story, descriptive essays do not always feature traditional topic sentences for every paragraph. But you can still use them to spearhead your main ideas and let your reader know where you are headed. Note how the topic sentence of Paragraph 6 does this.

out: a suicide bomber had driven a truck packed with explosives into the front gate of their base.

Paragraph 7

Coulter moved swiftly but with control. "You can't lose your head, you know. You gotta do what you're there to do." There was smoke and debris all around him, and in the distance he heard car alarms and other chaotic noises. He ran past bodies and body parts, trying just to focus on finding his team and establishing a security perimeter, as he had been instructed.

Paragraph 8

What descriptive details are found in Paragraph 8? What specific information is provided?

When he finally got beyond the main gate, he saw the damage. "It was total gore and carnage, that's the only way to describe it," he recalls. He saw dead people and wounded people. Their bodies were caked in mud, blood, and dust. The car that had delivered the blast was barely distinguishable. "You could tell it was once a car, but all that was left of it was parts of the engine in a big blown out ditch, like a crater," he said. Huge concrete walls that are intended to block such explosions had been "vaporized, totally turned to dust. Bigger chunks of debris were all over the place and you could see that they had killed several people who were walking past at that moment." Coulter and his team secured the area and coordinated with nearby aid stations to get supplies. He later learned the Taliban took responsibility for the attack. "It's just terrible because they're killing their own people, you know?"

Specific details help your reader more easily picture the subject you are writing about. Did the details in this essay help you imagine what Coulter's time as a soldier was like?

Paragraph 9

Coulter feels lucky that he was not killed or seriously wounded during his service. "I know a lot of guys who can't say the same," he says. He looks back on his tour in Afghanistan as one of the most important things he will ever do. "It was certainly an experience that has helped make me who I am, and I won't ever forget it."

Works Cited

Interview conducted by Scherer, Lauri S. 22 Oct. 2011.

Exercise 3A: Conducting an Interview

Model Essay Three, "The War in Afghanistan Through a Soldier's Eyes," was written after conducting an interview with Jared Coulter. When reporting on events that occur in your community, you will probably need to interview people to get critical information and opinions. Interviews allow you to get the story behind a participant's experiences, enabling you to provide a fuller picture of the event.

The key to a successful interview is asking the right questions. You want the respondent to answer in as much detail as possible so you can write an accurate, colorful, and interesting piece. Therefore, you should have a clear idea of what general pieces of information you want to find out from the respondent before you begin interviewing. The six classic journalist questions—who, what, when, where, why, and how—are an excellent place to begin. If you get answers to each of these questions, you will end up with a pretty good picture of the event that took place.

There are many ways to conduct an interview, but the following suggestions will help you get started:

Step One: Choose a setting with little distraction.
Avoid bright lights or loud noises, and make sure the person you are interviewing feels comfortable speaking to you. Professional settings such as offices, places of business, and homes are always appropriate settings for an interview. If it is a phone interview, be sure you can clearly hear what the person is saying (so do not conduct the interview on a cell phone while walking on a busy city block, for example).

Step Two: Explain who you are and what you intend to learn from the interview.
Identify yourself. For what publication are you writing? If you are writing for a school paper, identify the paper. If you are conducting research for an ongoing project, explain the project's goals and in what way you expect the interviewee can help you reach them. Indicate how

long you expect the interview to take, and get all contact information upfront.

Step Three: Ask specific questions, and start at the beginning. Make sure you ask at least two questions that address each of the following ideas: who, what, where, when, why and how. Who was involved in the event? What happened during the course of the event? Where did it take place? Specific questions will change depending on what type of event you are covering. Follow your instincts; if you don't know something or have a question, ask. The answer will likely yield good information that will enhance your report.

Step Four: Take notes.
Never rely on your memory when conducting an interview. Either type or jot down notes, or ask the interviewee's permission to record the interview.

Step Five: Verify quotes and information.
Before you write your report, it is important to go back to your source to double check key points of information. Also, you must run any quotes you intend to use by the source before you put them in your report. This is to make sure you heard the person accurately and are not misrepresenting his or her position.

Types of Questions to Ask During an Interview
Questions you will ask your interviewee tend to fall in a few basic categories.

Knowledge: what they know about the topic or event. This can include historical background, logistics, and outcomes of an event.

Sensory: what he or she saw, touched, heard, tasted or smelled. These details will help your readers more easily imagine the event you are reporting on.

Behavior: what motivated the person to become involved in the project or movement. What do they hope to gain by having their story publicized?

Opinions, values, and feelings: what the person thinks about the topic or event. These questions result in opinionated or personal statements that you, as an objective reporter, most likely will not make in your report.

Exercise 3B: Reporting on an Event

Reports show up in many publications—newspapers, magazines, journals, websites, and blogs are just some of the places people turn to read about events and activities happening in their community. Think about the type of event you'd like to report on. It could be a trip summary; a local or school event, such as a parade, speech, assembly, or rally; a sporting event; a party; or another experience in which people are coming together to get something done. Think next about the type of publication in which your report would best appear. Trip summaries, or travelogues, make great fodder for blogs; reports on school events such as sports or artistic performances are best featured in the school paper.

Before you report on an event, make sure you have done thorough research. Look over all notes from your interviews. Outline a road map for your essay to follow (see exercises in this book on how to outline an essay prior to writing it). Examine where quotations, information, and other details will fit best. After you understand and organize all the information you have collected, you are ready to write.

News reports tend to be objective, so make sure your writing style is impartial and matter-of-fact. Also, be sure to provide the reader with enough information to visualize the event but not so much that you bombard them with unnecessary or unrelated details. Use the other writing exercises found in this book—on using quotations, writing introductions and conclusions, and gathering research—to help you write the report. Then submit it for publication!

Write Your Own Descriptive Five-Paragraph Essay

Using the information in this book, write your own five-paragraph descriptive essay that deals with the war in Afghanistan. You can use the resources in this book for information about issues relating to this topic and how to structure this type of essay.

The following steps are suggestions for getting started:

Step One: Choose your topic.

The first step is to decide what topic to write your descriptive essay on. Is there anything that particularly fascinates you about war, the military, or Afghanistan? Is there an aspect of the topic you strongly support, or feel strongly against? Is there an issue you feel personally connected to or one that you would like to learn more about? Ask yourself such questions before selecting your essay topic. Refer to Appendix D: Sample Essay Topics if you need help selecting a topic.

Step Two: Write down questions and answers about the topic.

Before you begin writing, you will need to think carefully about what ideas your essay will contain. This is a process known as *brainstorming*. Brainstorming involves asking yourself questions and coming up with ideas to discuss in your essay. Possible questions that will help you with the brainstorming process include:

- Why is this topic important?
- Why should people be interested in this topic?
- How can I make this essay interesting to the reader?
- What question am I going to address in this paragraph or essay?
- What facts, ideas, or quotes can I use to support the answer to my question?

Questions especially for descriptive essays include:

- Have I chosen a compelling story or subject to examine or interview?
- Have I used vivid details?

- Have I made scenes, events, processes, and issues come alive for my reader?
- What qualities do my characters have? Are they interesting?
- Does my descriptive essay have a clear beginning, middle, and end?
- Does my essay evoke a particular emotion or response from the reader?

Step Three: Gather facts, ideas, and anecdotes related to your topic.

This book contains several places to find information about many aspects of military service and the war in Afghanistan, including the viewpoints and the appendices. In addition, you may want to research the books, articles, and websites listed in Section Three, or do additional research in your local library. You can also conduct interviews if you know someone who has a compelling story that would fit well in your essay.

Step Four: Develop a workable thesis statement.

Use what you have written down in steps two and three to help you articulate the main point or argument you want to make in your essay. It should be expressed in a clear sentence and make an arguable or supportable point.

Example:

More than a decade of war has taken its toll on soldiers deployed to Afghanistan.

This could be the thesis statement of a descriptive essay that argues in favor of ending the war because of the many tours of duty some soldiers have served. To support your argument, try to find a soldier to interview.

Step Five: Write an outline or diagram.

a. Write the thesis statement at the top of the outline.

b. Write roman numerals I, II, and III on the left side of the page with A, B, and C under each numeral.

c. Next to each roman numeral, write down the best ideas you came up with in step three. These should all directly relate to and support the thesis statement.

d. Next to each letter write down information that supports that particular idea.

Step Six: Write the three supporting paragraphs.

Use your outline to write the three supporting paragraphs. Write down the main idea of each paragraph in sentence form. Do the same thing for the supporting points of information. Each sentence should support the paragraph of the topic. Be sure you have relevant and interesting details, facts, and quotes. Use transitions when you move from idea to idea to keep the text fluid and smooth. Sometimes, although not always, paragraphs can include a concluding or summary sentence that restates the paragraph's argument.

Step Seven: Write the introduction and conclusion.

See Exercise 2B for information on writing introductions and conclusions.

Step Eight: Read and rewrite.

As you read, check your essay for the following:

- ✔ Does the essay maintain a consistent tone?
- ✔ Do all paragraphs reinforce your general thesis?
- ✔ Do all paragraphs flow from one to the other, or do you need to add transition words or phrases?
- ✔ Have you quoted from reliable, authoritative, and interesting sources?
- ✔ Is there a sense of progression throughout the essay?
- ✔ Does the essay get bogged down in too much detail or irrelevant material?
- ✔ Does your introduction grab the reader's attention?
- ✔ Does your conclusion reflect back on any previously discussed material and give the essay a sense of closure?
- ✔ Are there any spelling or grammatical errors?

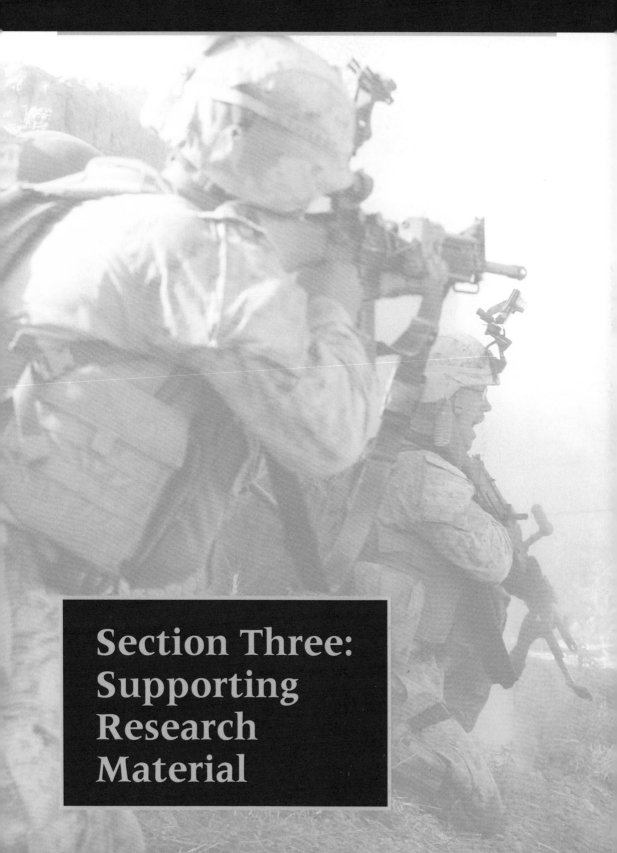

Section Three:
Supporting
Research
Material

Timeline of Facts for the War in Afghanistan

Editor's Note: The facts contained in this timeline can be used in reports to back up important points or claims.

September 2001

The United States is attacked by nineteen al Qaeda operatives, fifteen of whom are Saudi Arabian. It is determined that the operatives trained in al Qaeda terrorist camps in Afghanistan. President George W. Bush demands that the Taliban, the rulers of Afghanistan at the time, turn over al Qaeda leader Osama bin Laden or face war with the United States.

October 2001

With help from the British, the United States launches Operation Enduring Freedom, a bombing campaign intended to root out al Qaeda and Taliban leaders in Afghanistan. Polls show that 94 percent of Americans support the air strikes; 75 percent favor sending in ground troops if necessary.

November 2001

The Northern Alliance—a group of Afghan fighters who are anti-Taliban—breaks through Taliban positions in the city of Mazar-e Sharif. Together, they and coalition forces take the Afghan capital, Kabul.

November 25, 2001

CIA officer Johnny "Mike" Spann is killed during a prison uprising in Mazar-e-Sharif, becoming the first US combat casualty of the campaign. American John Walker Lindh is found fighting with Taliban forces.

December 2001

Approximately two hundred al Qaeda fighters are killed in the caves of Tora Bora in Afghanistan.

The Taliban are uprooted from the major city of Kandahar, but Taliban leader Mohammed Omar and al Qaeda leader Osama bin Laden escape.

Hamid Karzai, an ethnic Pashtun who leads one of the largest tribes in southern Afghanistan, is sworn in as head of a new interim government.

By year's end, 12 US soldiers have been killed in the war.

February 2002

US forces begin training a new Afghan national army.

November 2002

The US Congress approves $2.3 billion in reconstruction funds and an additional $1 billion for expansion of the NATO-led International Security Assistance Force (ISAF) in Afghanistan.

December 2002

By year's end, 69 coalition soldiers have been killed in the war, bringing the war's total to 81 casualties.

January 2003

The United Nations estimates that more than 4 million Afghan refugees have been created by the war.

March 2003

The United States begins combat operations in Iraq, a war that will overshadow Afghanistan until 2009.

A CBS News/*New York Times* poll finds that 76 percent of Americans think the war in Afghanistan is going very well or somewhat well; 14 percent think it is going badly or somewhat badly; 10 percent are unsure.

April 2003
NATO takes over command of security forces in Afghanistan.

December 2003
By year's end, 57 coalition soldiers have been killed in the war, bringing the war's total to 138 casualties.

October 2004
Elections are held in Afghanistan. Hamid Karzai becomes the nation's first democratically elected president.

December 2004
By year's end, 59 coalition soldiers have been killed in the war, bringing the war's total to 197 casualties.

May 2005
US forces are accused of abusing prisoners at detention centers in Afghanistan.

September 2005
For the first time in thirty years, parliamentary and provincial elections are held in Afghanistan.

December 2005
By year's end, 131 coalition soldiers have been killed in the war, bringing the war's total to 328 casualties.

May 2006
Anti-US protests erupt in Kabul after a US military vehicle crashes and kills several people.

July 2006
NATO troops take over military operations in the south, where severe fighting persists because of a strong Taliban presence there.

September 2006

A CNN/Opinion Research Corporation poll finds that 50 percent of Americans favor the war while 48 percent oppose it and 2 percent are unsure.

December 2006

By year's end, 191 coalition soldiers have been killed in the war, bringing the war's total to 519 casualties.

May 2007

The Taliban's most senior military commander, Mullah Dadullah, is killed during fighting with US and Afghan forces.

August 2007

The United Nations says that opium production in Afghanistan is at an all-time high since the war began.

December 2007

By year's end, 232 coalition soldiers have been killed in the war, bringing the war's total to 751 casualties. The United Nations reports that 1,523 Afghan civilians were killed in 2007.

June 2008

Taliban fighters free twelve hundred prisoners, including four hundred Taliban prisoners of war, in an assault on a Kandahar jail. Taliban attacks on coalition forces and civilians intensify throughout the summer.

August 2008

A CBS News/*New York Times* poll finds that 28 percent of Americans think the war is going very well or some-what well; 58 percent think it is going badly or somewhat badly; 14 percent are unsure.

December 2008

By year's end, 294 coalition soldiers have been killed in the war, bringing the war's total to 1,045 casualties. The United Nations reports that 2,118 Afghan civilians were killed in 2008.

January 2009

Thousands of US troops move into two key provinces in east Afghanistan as part of the strategy of outgoing administration of US president George W. Bush.

February 2009

President Barack Obama orders seventeen thousand additional US troops to be sent to Afghanistan as part of an effort to refocus attention on the war there.

March 2009

Obama announces a new strategy and plans to send four thousand additional troops to Afghanistan.

May 2009

The United States shifts from a conventional strategy to a counterinsurgency one aimed at reducing civilian deaths.

June 2009

US general Stanley McChrystal is put in charge of international troops in Afghanistan.

August 20, 2009

Afghanistan holds its second presidential election since the start of the war, but it is marred by accusations of corruption and fraud.

September 2009

A CNN/Opinion Research Corporation poll finds that just 39 percent of Americans favor the war while 58 percent oppose it—the most since the start of the war.

October 2009

The Obama administration says it will hold off sending new troops to Afghanistan until a legitimate and credible government can be established there.

Fifty-three US troops are killed in Afghanistan—the most in any month since the war began in October 2001.

November 2009

Hamid Karzai is certified as president of Afghanistan for another term.

December 2009

President Obama commits thirty thousand more US troops to Afghanistan, to join the sixty-eight thousand already in place. He establishes July 2011 as a goal for beginning troop withdrawal.

June 2010

General Stanley McChrystal resigns as commander of US forces in Afghanistan after making controversial statements criticizing the Obama administration. General David Petraeus takes his place.

May 1, 2011

Osama bin Laden is killed in Pakistan by US special forces.

June 2011

President Obama outlines a plan to withdraw ten thousand troops by the end of 2011. A Pew Research poll shows the majority of Americans—56 percent—continue to oppose the war.

October 7, 2011

The ten-year anniversary of the war is marked. A decade of war has cost $444 billion and thousands of lives.

November 30, 2011

To date, 1,846 American soldiers and 973 international troops have been killed in the war in Afghanistan, bringing the war's total to 2,819 casualties.

Summer 2012

Thirty-three thousand American troops are slated for withdrawal by summer of 2012, according to President Obama's June 2011 initiative.

December 2014

NATO is expected to hand over Afghanistan's national security to the Afghan National Army.

Finding and Using Sources of Information

No matter what type of essay you are writing, it is necessary to find information to support your point of view. You can use sources such as books, magazine articles, newspaper articles, and online articles.

Using Books and Articles

You can find books and articles in a library by using the library's computer or cataloging system. If you are not sure how to use these resources, ask a librarian to help you. You can also use a computer to find many magazine articles and other articles written specifically for the Internet.

You are likely to find a lot more information than you can possibly use in your essay, so your first task is to narrow it down to what is likely to be most usable. Look at book and article titles. Look at book chapter titles, and examine the book's index to see if it contains information on the specific topic you want to write about. For example, if you want to write about the cost of the war in Afghanistan and you find a book about military spending, check the chapter titles and index to be sure it contains information about Afghanistan before you bother to check out the book.

For a five-paragraph essay, you do not need a great deal of supporting information, so quickly try to narrow down your materials to a few good books and magazine or Internet articles. You do not need dozens. You might even find that one or two good books or articles contain all the information you need.

You probably do not have time to read an entire book, so find the chapters or sections that relate to your topic, and skim these. When you find useful information, copy it onto a note card or notebook. You should look for supporting facts, statistics, quotations, and examples.

Using the Internet

When you select your supporting information, it is important that you evaluate its source. This is especially important with information you find on the Internet. Because nearly anyone can put information on the Internet, there is as much bad information as good information. Before using Internet information—or any information—try to determine whether the source is reliable. Is the author or Internet site sponsored by a legitimate organization? Is it from a government source? Does the author have any special knowledge or training relating to the topic you are looking up? Does the article give any indication of where its information comes from?

Using Your Supporting Information

When you use supporting information from a book, article, interview or other source, there are three important things to remember:

1. *Make it clear whether you are using a direct quotation or a paraphrase.* If you copy information directly from your source, you are quoting it. You must put quotation marks around the information, and tell where the information comes from. If you put the information in your own words, you are paraphrasing it.

2. *Use the information fairly.* Be careful to use supporting information so that it means what the author intended it to mean. For example, it is unfair to quote an author as saying, "The war in Afghanistan is unwinnable" when the author's text actually says, "The war in Afghanistan is unwinnable only if it is unsupported and underfunded." This is called taking information out of context and is using supporting evidence unfairly.

3. *Give credit where credit is due.* Giving credit is known as citing. You must use citations when you use someone else's information, but not every piece of supporting information needs a citation.
   - If the supporting information is general knowledge—that is, if it can be found in many sources (e.g., the distance around the globe)— you do not have to cite your source.
   - If you directly quote a source, you must cite it.
   - If you paraphrase information from a specific source, you must cite it.

If you do not use citations where you should, you are *plagiarizing*—or stealing—someone else's work.

Citing Your Sources

There are a number of ways to cite your sources. Your teacher will probably want you to do it in one of three ways:
- Informal: As in the example in many of the model essays presented in Section Two of this book, tell where you got the information as you present it in the text of your essay.
- Informal list: At the end of your essay, place an unnumbered list of all the sources you used. This tells the reader where, in general, your information came from.
- Formal: Use numbered footnotes or endnotes. Footnotes are placed at the bottom of the page that they appear on in the text whereas endnotes are generally placed at the end of an essay, although they may be placed elsewhere depending on your teacher's requirements.

Using MLA Style to Create a Works Cited List

You will probably need to create a list of works cited for your paper. These include materials that you quoted from, relied heavily on, or consulted to write your paper. There are several different ways to structure these references. The following examples are based on Modern Language Association (MLA) style, one of the major citation styles used by writers.

Book Entries

For most book entries you will need the author's name, the book's title, where it was published, what company published it, and the year it was published. This information is usually found on the inside of the book. Variations on book entries include the following:

A Book by a Single Author:
　　Axworthy, Michael. *A History of Iran: Empire of the Mind.* New York: Basic, 2008.

Two or More Books by the Same Author:
Pollan, Michael. *In Defense of Food: An Eater's Manifesto.* New York: Penguin, 2009.
　　———. *The Omnivore's Dilemma.* New York: Penguin, 2006.

A Book by Two or More Authors:
Ronald, Pamela C., and R. W. Adamchak. *Tomorrow's Table: Organic Farming, Genetics, and the Future of Food.* New York: Oxford UP, 2008.

A Book with an Editor
Scherer, Lauri S., ed. *Introducing Issues with Opposing Viewpoints: War.* Detroit: Greenhaven, 2009.

Periodical and Newspaper Entries

Entries for sources found in periodicals and newspapers are cited a bit differently than books. For one, these sources usually have a title and a publication name. They also may have specific dates and page numbers. Unlike book entries, you do not need to list where newspapers or periodicals are published or what company publishes them.

An Article from a Periodical:
Hannum, William H., Gerald E. Marsh, and George S. Stanford. "Smarter Use of Nuclear Waste," *Scientific American* Dec. 2005: 84–91.

An Anonymous Article from a Periodical:
"The Chinese Disease? The Rapid Spread of Syphilis in China." *Global Agenda* 14 Jan. 2007.

An Article from a Newspaper:
Weiss, Rick. "Can Food from Cloned Animals Be Called Organic?" *Washington Post* 29 Jan. 2008: A06.

Internet Sources

To document a source you found online, try to provide as much information on it as possible, including the author's name, the title of the document, date of publication or of last revision, the URL, and the date you accessed the information.

A Web Source:
De Seno, Tommy. "*Roe vs. Wade* and the Rights of the Father." The Fox Forum.com 22 Jan. 2009. Web. 20 May 2009. < http://foxforum.blogs.foxnews.com /2009/01/22/deseno_roe_wade/ >

Your teacher will tell you exactly how information should be cited in your essay. Generally, the very least information needed is the original author's name and the name of the article or other publication.

Be sure you know exactly what information your teacher requires before you start looking for your supporting information so that you know what information to include with your notes.

Sample Essay Topics on the War in Afghanistan

Afghanistan Is a Just War

Afghanistan Is Not a Just War

Important Progress Has Been Made in Afghanistan

The War in Afghanistan Is a Complete Disaster

The United States Can Win in Afghanistan

The United States Cannot Win in Afghanistan

The War in Afghanistan Is Similar to the War in Vietnam

The War in Afghanistan Is Not Like the War in Vietnam

The Taliban Threaten Afghanistan and the Rest of the World

The Taliban Do Not Threaten Afghanistan nor the Rest of the World

Afghanistan Can Become a Democracy

Afghanistan Is Not Likely to Become a Democracy

Women Must Be Respected If Democracy Is to Work in Afghanistan

Afghanistan Suffers from Corrupt Elections

Afghanistan's Elections Are a Sign of Progress

The United States Should Leave Afghanistan

The United States Should Not Leave Afghanistan

The United States Should Commit to Afghanistan for Decades

The United States Should Withdraw from Afghanistan Immediately

The United States Should Send More Troops to Afghanistan

The United States Should Not Send More Troops to Afghanistan

The United States Should Focus on Helping the Afghan People

The Mission in Afghanistan Must Remain Military

Osama bin Laden's Death Should Lead to a US Withdrawal from Afghanistan

Osama bin Laden's Death Should Not Lead to a US Withdrawal from Afghanistan

Non-US Troops Should Immediately Leave Afghanistan

Non-US Troops Should Stay in Afghanistan

Descriptive Essay Topics

The Toll of Decades of War on Afghanistan

A Woman's Life in Afghanistan

Life in Kabul

The Life of a Soldier in Afghanistan

The War's Effect on American Soldiers and Their Families

Military Spending in Afghanistan

The War in Afghanistan Has Improved Conditions for Afghan Women and Children

Organizations to Contact

The editor has compiled the following list of organizations concerned with the issues debated in this book. The descriptions are derived from materials provided by the organizations. All have publications or information available for interested readers. The list was compiled on the date of publication of the present volume; the information provided here may change. Be aware that many organizations take several weeks or longer to respond to queries, so allow as much time as possible.

Afghan Women's Network (AWN)
Karta Parwan Square, House #22
Kabul, Afghanistan
website: www.afghanwomensnetwork.af

AWN is the only umbrella entity for women's/gender-based organizations in Afghanistan. It comprises seventy-two organizations with a total of three thousand members in both Pakistan and Afghanistan. AWN is a nongovernmental organization that works to empower Afghan women and ensure their equal participation in Afghan society.

Afghan Women's Organization
789 Don Mills Rd., Ste. 312
Toronto, ON M3C 1T5
Canada
(416) 588-3585
website: www.afghanwomen.org

This organization was created to address the unique needs of Afghan women and children in the Greater Toronto Area and even as far away as Afghanistan and Pakistan. It is dedicated to assisting Afghan women in all aspects of integration and adaptation to Canadian life; encouraging and motivating Afghan women to participate in and contribute to life in Canada; encouraging and promoting skill building and development among Afghan women; developing a community support network for women; promoting English language development; and organizing and implementing programs to educate and empower young Afghans to cope with personal, cultural, and social issues.

American Enterprise Institute (AEI)
1150 Seventeenth St. NW
Washington, DC 20036
(202) 862-5800 • fax: (202) 862-7177
website: www.aei.org

The American Enterprise Institute for Public Policy Research is a scholarly research institute that is dedicated to preserving limited government, private enterprise, and a strong foreign policy and national defense. It publishes books, including *Democratic Realism: An American Foreign Policy for a Unipolar World* and *The Islamic Paradox: Shiite Clerics, Sunni Fundamentalists, and the Coming of Arab Democracy*, as well as a bimonthly magazine, *American Enterprise*.

The Brookings Institution
1775 Massachusetts Ave. NW
Washington, DC 20036
(202) 797-6000 • fax: (202) 797-6004
e-mail: brookinfo@brook.edu
website: www.brookings.org

The institution, founded in 1927, is a think tank that conducts research and education in foreign policy, economics, government, and the social sciences. In 2001 it began America's Response to Terrorism, a project that provides briefings and analysis to the public and which is featured on the institution's website. It publishes the quarterly

Brookings Review, periodic *Policy Briefs,* and books on troubled countries, including Afghanistan.

Center for Strategic and International Studies (CSIS)

1800 K St. NW, Ste. 400
Washington, DC 20006
(202) 887-0200 • fax: (202) 775-3199
website: www.csis.org

CSIS works to provide world leaders with strategic insights and policy options on current and emerging global issues. Numerous reports related to the war in Afghanistan can be downloaded from its website.

Council on Foreign Relations

58 E. Sixty-Eighth St.
New York, NY 10021
(212) 434-9400 • fax: (212) 434-9800
e-mail: communications@cfr.org
website: www.cfr.org

The council researches the international aspects of American economic and political policies. Its journal *Foreign Affairs,* published five times a year, provides analysis on global conflicts, including the ongoing one in Afghanistan.

Hoover Institution

Stanford University
Stanford, CA 94305-6010
(650) 723-1754 • fax: (650) 723-1687
website: www.hoover.org

The Hoover Institution is a public policy research center devoted to advanced study of politics, economics, and political economy—both domestic and foreign—as well as international affairs. As well as a newsletter and special reports, the institution publishes the quarterly *Hoover Digest,* which often includes articles on Afghanistan and the war on terrorism.

Human Rights Watch (HRW)
485 Fifth Ave.
New York, NY 10017-6104
(212) 972-8400 • fax: (212) 972-0905
e-mail: hrwnyc@hrw.org • website: www.hrw.org

Human Rights Watch regularly investigates human rights abuses in over seventy countries around the world. It promotes civil liberties and defends freedom of thought, due process, and the equal protection under the law. Its goal is to hold governments accountable for human rights violations they commit against individuals because of the individuals' political, ethnic, or religious affiliations. It publishes a wealth of information about Afghanistan, including current information, background information, and regular human rights reports.

The National Endowment for Democracy
1101 Fifteenth St. NW, Ste. 700
Washington, DC 20005
(202) 293-9072 • fax: (202) 223-6042
e-mail: info@ned.org • website: www.ned.org

The National Endowment for Democracy is a private non-profit organization created in 1983 to strengthen democratic institutions around the world through nongovernmental efforts. It publishes the bimonthly periodical the *Journal of Democracy*.

North Atlantic Treaty Organization (NATO)/ International Security Assistance Force (ISAF)
Blvd. Leopold III
1110 Brussels
Belgium
website: www.nato.int/ISAF

NATO is an alliance of twenty-eight countries from North America and Europe committed to fulfilling the goals of the North Atlantic Treaty, which was signed in 1949. NATO offers a forum for member countries to consult on pressing security issues around the world and take joint action in addressing them. NATO is in charge of the International Security Assistance Force, the body of coalition troops in Afghanistan.

Revolutionary Association of the Women of Afghanistan (RAWA)
PO Box 374
Quetta, Pakistan
e-mail: rawa@rawa.org • website: www.rawa.org

RAWA was established in Kabul, Afghanistan, in 1977 as an independent political/social organization of Afghan women fighting for human rights and for social justice in Afghanistan. RAWA continues to fight for freedom, democracy, and women's rights in Afghanistan. It is the publisher of a bilingual (Persian/Pashtu) magazine, *Payam-e-Zan*, which means "woman's message." Its website contains news updates and other information pertaining to women's rights in Afghanistan.

UN Development Programme in Afghanistan
1 United Nations Plaza
New York, NY 10017
(212) 906-5317
website: www.undp.org.af

The programme is the United Nations' global development network, helping countries build solutions to the challenges of democratic governance, poverty reduction, crisis prevention and recovery, energy and environment, information and communications technology, and HIV/AIDS. The United Nations Development Programme has been present in Afghanistan for more than fifty years and works to support the people of Afghanistan as they face new challenges and move their country forward.

Bibliography

Books

Eric Blehm, *The Only Thing Worth Dying For: How Eleven Green Berets Fought for a New Afghanistan*. New York: HarperPerennial, 2011.

Rusty Bradley and Kevin Maurer, *Lions of Kandahar: The Story of a Fight Against All Odds*. New York: Bantam Books, 2011.

Seth G. Jones, *In the Graveyard of Empires: America's War in Afghanistan*. New York: W.W. Norton, 2010.

Joe LeBleu, *Long Rifle: A Sniper's Story in Iraq and Afghanistan*. Guilford, CT: Lyons Press, 2008.

Suraya Sadeed and Damien Lewis, *Forbidden Lessons in a Kabul Guesthouse: The True Story of a Woman Who Risked Everything to Bring Hope to Afghanistan*. New York: Voice, 2011.

Brian Glyn Williams, *Afghanistan Declassified: A Guide to America's Longest War*. Philadelphia: University of Pennsylvania Press, 2011.

Periodicals and Internet Sources

Peter Bergen, "Winning the Good War," *Washington Monthly*, July/August 2009. www.washingtonmonthly.com/features/2009/0907.bergen.html.

David Brooks, "The Winnable War," *New York Times*, March 27, 2009, p. A29. www.nytimes.com/2009/03/27/opinion/27brooks.html.

Prajwal Ciryam, "Bin Laden's Death Is the Worst Reason to Leave Afghanistan," Partisans.org, May 12, 2011. www.partisans.org/2011/05/bin-ladens-death-is-the-worst-reason-to-leave-afghanistan/.

Daily Telegraph (London), "Osama bin Laden Dead: War on Terror Is Not Yet Won," May 3, 2011. www.telegraph.co.uk/news/worldnews/northamerica/usa/8488415/

Osama-bin-Laden-dead-war-on-terror-is-not-yet-won.html.

Yochi J. Dreazen, "With Bin Laden Dead, Should the War in Afghanistan Die with Him?," *National Journal,* May 3, 2011. http://nationaljournal.com/with-bin-laden-dead-should-the-war-in-afghanistan-die-with-him--20110503.

Georgie Hanlan, "The Afghanistan War, Through the Eyes of a Soldier's Wife," *Christian Science Monitor,* April 26, 2010. www.csmonitor.com/Commentary/Opinion/2010/0426/The-Afghanistan-war-through-the-eyes-of-a-soldier-s-wife.

Max Hastings, "Don't Fool Yourselves—Afghanistan Is an Unwinnable War," *Daily Mail* (London), November 6, 2009. www.dailymail.co.uk/debate/columnists/article-1225626/MAX-HASTINGS-Dont-fool--Afghanistan-unwinnable-war.html.

Mike Honda, "Time to Draw Down in Afghanistan," *Hill,* May 10, 2011, p. 32. http://thehill.com/opinion/op-ed/160079-time-to-draw-down-in-afghanistan.

Ann Jones, "In Afghanistan, a Woman's Place Is at the Peace Table," *Los Angeles Times,* January 13, 2011. http://articles.latimes.com/2011/jan/13/opinion/la-oe-jones-afghanistan-women-20110113-11.

Independent (London), "An Unwinnable War," August 1, 2010. www.independent.co.uk/opinion/leading-articles/leading-article-an-unwinnable-war-2040554.html.

Frederick W. Kagan, "Afghanistan Is Not Vietnam," *Newsweek,* February 10, 2009. www.newsweek.com/2009/02/10/afghanistan-is-not-vietnam.html.

Gayle Tzemach Lemmon, "Myths About 'Unwinnable' Afghanistan," CNN.com, February 17, 2011. http://articles.cnn.com/2011-02-17/opinion/lemmon.afghanistan_1_afghanistan-king-amanullah-afghan-women?_s=PM:OPINION.

E. Thomas McClanahan, "An Afghanistan Scale-Down Road Map," *Kansas City (MO) Star,* March 20, 2011. www

.mcclatchydc.com/2011/03/20/110391/commentary
-an-afghanistan-scale.html.

Paul Miller, "Afghanistan Is Not Vietnam," *Foreign Policy*,
October 7, 2010. http://shadow.foreignpolicy.com
/posts/2010/10/07/afghanistan_is_not_vietnam.

Anne Penketh, "Five Reasons to Leave Afghanistan." *Hill*,
May 18, 2011, p. 16. http://thehill.com/opinion/op-ed
/161789-five-reasons-to-leave-afghanistan.

Doug Saunders, "We're Killing the Afghans We Should Be
Speaking To," *Globe & Mail* (Toronto), May 30, 2011.
http://m.theglobeandmail.com/news/opinions/opinion
/were-killing-the-afghans-we-should-be-speaking-to
/article2037846/?service = mobile.

Theodore Sorenson, "America's Next Unwinnable War,"
The Daily Beast, October 30, 2009. www.thedaily
beast.com/blogs-and-stories/2009-10-30/americas
-next-unwinnable-war/.

Times (London), "Abandon the Military Status Quo, Not
the Wars," May 16, 2011, p. 18.

Times of Trenton (NJ), "Osama bin Laden Death Should
Hasten Troop Withdrawal from Afghanistan," May 10,
2011. www.nj.com/times-opinion/index.ssf/2011/05
/editorial_osama_bin_laden_deat.html.

Cenk Uygur, "Bin Laden Dead—War Was Not the
Answer," *Huffington Post*, May 2, 2011. www.huffing
tonpost.com/cenk-uygur/bin-laden-dead-war-was
-no_b_856170.html.

Stephen Vizinczey, "Afghanistan Is an Unwinnable War,
and Our Leaders Know It," *Daily Telegraph* (London),
August 2, 2010. www.telegraph.co.uk/news/world
news/asia/afghanistan/7923059/Afghanistan-is-an
-unwinnable-war-and-our-leaders-know-it.html.

Washington Times, "Afghanistan Is a Winnable War,"
June 14, 2009. www.washingtontimes.com/news/2009
/jun/14/afghanistan-is-a-winnable-war/.

George F. Will, "Time for the U.S. to Get Out of
Afghanistan," *Washington Post*, September 1, 2009.
www.washingtonpost.com/wp-dyn/content/article
/2009/08/31/AR2009083102912.html.

Websites

Afghanistan Online (www.afghan-web.com/woman). This site contains articles, poems, and essays describing the plight of Afghanistan's women.

Afghan News Network (www.afghannews.net). A collection of news related to Afghanistan from a wide variety of major news sources that is updated regularly throughout the day.

BBC Country Profile of Afghanistan (http://news.bbc .co.uk/2/hi/south_asia /country_profiles/1162668 .stm). This site offers maps, statistics, facts, and other current information on Afghanistan's people, land, government, and more.

CIA World Factbook, Afghanistan (www.cia.gov/library /publications/the-world-factbook/geos/af.html). This site, maintained by the CIA, contains up-to-date demographic information on Afghanistan. Students will find its maps and facts useful when doing reports and papers on this topic.

iCasualties—Afghanistan (http://icasualties.org/oef). iCasualties tracks the number of dead in global conflicts. On this page it offers up-to-date information on military fatalities broken down by nationality, date, province, and more.

Rethink Afghanistan (http://rethinkafghanistan.com). This site, maintained by the Brave New Foundation, features video clips that argue point-by-point against the war in Afghanistan.

World Health Organization—Afghanistan (www.who .int/countries/afg/en). The World Health Organization is the directing and coordinating authority for health within the United Nations system. Its Afghanistan site offers demographic information and statistics on life expectancy, morbidity, disease outbreaks, and other health-related news in that country.

Index

Picture Credits

About the Editor

Lauri S. Scherer earned her bachelor's degree in religion and political science from Vassar College in Poughkeepsie, New York. Her studies there focused on political Islam. Scherer has worked as a nonfiction writer, a newspaper journalist, and a book editor for more than ten years. She has extensive experience in both academic and professional settings.

Scherer is the founder of LSF Editorial, a writing and editing company in San Diego, California. She has edited and authored numerous publications for Greenhaven Press on controversial social issues such as Islam, genetically modified food, women's rights, school shootings, gay marriage, and Iraq. Every book in the *Writing the Critical Essay* series has been under her direction or editorship, and she has personally written more than twenty titles in the series. She was instrumental in the creation of the series, and played a critical role in its conception and development.